Bottles and Pot Lids

A Collector's Guide

MILLER'S

Bottles and Pot Lids

A Collector's Guide

Alan Blakeman

MILLER'S BOTTLES AND POT LIDS: A COLLECTOR'S GUIDE
by Alan Blakeman

First published in Great Britain in 2002 by Miller's, a division of
Mitchell Beazley, imprints of Octopus Publishing Group Ltd,
2–4 Heron Quays, London E14 4JP

Miller's is a registered trademark of Octopus Publishing Group Ltd

Copyright © Octopus Publishing Group Ltd 2002

Commissioning Editor **Anna Sanderson**
Executive Art Editor **Rhonda Fisher**
Editorial Assistant **Rose Hudson**
Designer **Louise Griffiths, Victoria Bevan**
Editor **Selina Mumford**
Proofreader **Miranda Stonor**
Indexer **Sue Farr**
Production **Angela Couchman**
Jacket photography by **Steve Tanner**

The publishers will be grateful for any information that will assist them
in keeping future editions up to date. While every care has been taken
in the preparation of this book, neither the author nor the publisher
can accept any liability for any consequence arising from the use
thereof, or the information contained therein. Values shown should be
used as a guide only as prices vary according to geographical location
and demand.

ISBN 1 84000 539 4

A CIP catalogue record for this book is available from the British Library
Set in Bembo, Frutiger and Shannon
Produced by Toppan Printing Co., (HK) Ltd.
Printed and bound in China

Jacket illustrations, front cover, clockwise from top: Corbett's Irish
Whiskey water jug, c.1880–1900, **£400–600/$600–900**; Rock Blue bottle,
c.1900, **£60–80/$90–120**; Yarmouth Bloater Paste pot lid, c.1880–1900,
£100–120/$150–180
Half-title page: French-made bisque statuette for Mrs S. A. Allen's World
Famed Hair Restorer, c.1870-1890, **£1,200–1,500/$1,800–2,200**
Contents page: Saltglaze monk inkwell, c.1830-40,
£400–500/$600–750; green glass Warner's Safe Nervine, c. 1890-1910,
£60–80/$90–120

contents

6   How to start

8   Digging

10   Breweriana

12   Black glass

14   Dairy items

16   Doulton

18   Fire grenades

20   Ginger beer

24   Go-withs

26   In the bathroom

28   Pottery inks

30   Glass inks

32   Kitchenalia

34   Mineral waters

38   Ointment pots

40   Poison bottles

42   Pot lids

46   Quack cures

48   Pharmacy

50   Early stoneware

52   Water filters

54   Water jugs

56   Whisky crocks

58   Fakes & forgeries

59   Glossary

59   What to read

60   Clubs, shows, & magazines

61   Where to buy and see

62   Index

64   Acknowledgments

How to start

Investigating "how we used to live" is inextricably linked with bottles and collectable "go-withs" (see pp.24–5) of a bygone age. Few fail to be captivated by the attractive coloured glass receptacles of yesteryear which form the basis of this fascinating and well-established field of collecting. Other items include prettily transferred pottery, quack cures, ingenious patent designs, or hand-thrown saltglazed stoneware pots made 100–150 years ago. All of this material is readily available if you know where to look, and although some expensive examples are included in this book, prices can start from as little as a pound (or dollar).

The actual term "bottle collecting" is something of a misnomer, as it does not fully reflect the enormous variety and breadth this field offers. Let me explain. Imagine filling your weekly shopping trolley at a supermarket. Possibly, on your way out, you might spot a cut-out lifesize pop star promotion for a chocolate bar, or maybe pick up a printed flier about a celebrity making a forthcoming appearance. All that material: the empty packets, jars, cut-out posters, and fliers will years later reflect eating, drinking, and social habits of a particular era.

The Industrial Revolution fuelled the momentum of a rapidly expanding market economy, witnessing a mass exodus of land workers to the new factories, mills, and industrial centres in both Britain and around the world. Packaging of all manner of products for home consumption throughout this period relied heavily upon vibrant glass colours, unusual and eye-catching shapes, unique designs, and weird and wonderful patent ideas. All were born from one of the most imaginative and inventive periods in history.

Most items in this book span the period 1880–1920. While it is possible to visit any antique mall or fair, and purchase many items

Transferred stoneware ginger beer bottle, Swansea, c.1910–20, **£25–30/$37–45**

from this book, I would suggest you proceed with caution. As with all other collecting areas, this one can be fraught with problems; a minefield to the unwary. Specialist fairs, reputable dealers, and established salerooms can provide a more reliable purchasing "parachute", offering benefits beyond sensibly priced goods.

It is a good idea to read around the subject, getting a "feel" for the kind of material that is, and is not, collected. Shrewd collectors move with wisdom, avoiding jumping in at the deep end and buying the proverbial pig in a poke! Many choose to specialize in a particular field, such as soft drink containers for aerated mineral water or ginger beers, pot lids for a multitude of products, early black glass or handmade pottery, pharmacy-related products, or alcoholic drink containers. The list is more extensive than even this book can suggest.

Marble stoppered codd, excellent condition, c.1870, **£2–5/$3–7**

Condition is a personal choice. Something costing £50/$75 when perfect may be worth less than half if damaged. It is recommended you collect what you personally find interesting and attractive. However, it cannot be ignored that a large or serious collection can form a considerable outlay, and that for future resale purposes, good condition is a prerequisite.

Bargains are out there for the diligent hunter. Even digging sites remain and have something to offer. Ultimately, the bottle hobby can be a highly enjoyable one, with fascinating background information providing an increased knowledge of how our ancestors lived.

Ceramic pot lid with matching base, "Woods Areca Nut Tooth Paste", c.1880–1920 (sold worldwide, **£8–12/$12–18**)

For less than £10/$15 a time it is still easy to obtain many local bottles, around 100 years old. Most of the companies are now defunct, but local library research will reveal much about the past lives of the cherished empties.

Modern backlit display cabinets enhance the dramatic effect of coloured glass or ceramics, and provide protection against accidental damage. Shelving across an alcove is another effective way to display the items. However, one of the beauties of bottles is the superb way they give ambience to kitchens, hallways, or bathrooms. Advertising showcards, enamel signs, and old mirrors all add to the overall effect of period recreation.

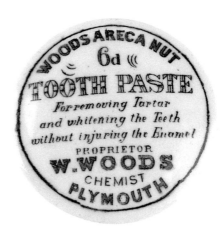

Prices

All items valued here relate to perfect specimens. Damage of any kind can make a large difference. Specialist shows and auctions are the surest sources of acquisition, although antique fairs, and car boot and garage sales are also good hunting grounds. The sterling/dollar conversion is calculated at £1 = $1.50 (adjust the dollar value as necessary to accord with current exchange rates).

Digging

The lure

The prospect of digging up items of pottery and glass over 100 years old, for free, is enormously exciting: akin to finding buried treasure. Not all discoveries from Victorian and Edwardian rubbish dumps are of high value, but the glisten from the ash banking, and finding out what it is, cannot be fully appreciated until you have been there and done it. The adrenalin rush and even the disappointment upon finding broken pieces are all part of the allure.

With luck, and some research, it is possible to gather a selection of antique empties. The rubbish our ancestors threw away tells us much about how they lived, through what they ate and drank. Organized refuse disposal, like so much from our past, was another clever Victorian concept. Empty bottles and jars joined all the other paraphernalia of our ancestors' waste, which was tossed into the daily ashes from the coal fire and then carried out of town by cart or rail, dumped, and finally capped with soil and grassed over. Small villages often filled old quarries, ponds, and such like.

Today, it is possible to rediscover these areas and unearth previously discarded items, many in good condition. After 80 to 100 years underground, a wipe or a wash in warm soapy water is all that is needed to make the pieces glisten and gleam as they did the day they were made.

Library research can help in finding these long-forgotten sites. One method involves comparing old and new maps, as this can reveal where clay pits, ponds, lime kilns, quarries, etc have been filled in. An old map may show a site marked as "a quarry" and if the later map does not show it presumably it was filled in.

There can be rich pickings, as the pages of this book reveal, but it is very much the social

history and the variety of objects to be found which is the real attraction. The hobby is over 30 years old, and the easier to find locations will most probably have been dug by now. Some people have refound such "dug out" sites, and carefully redug to systematically find missed patches. Always keep an eye on any building work in your local area, as often builders cut through old rubbish dumps, especially in the larger towns and cities.

A local Bottle Club (see p 60) can provide instant, valuable advice, and possibly even a chance to dig with an experienced member. If you are successful in finding an untouched site, remember that all land belongs to someone and permission must be obtained. Locating

Expect to find much broken material; cast away with household rubbish, items may have been buried for over 80 years. Left: boot blacking jar, c.1900–20; bottom: Vinolia pot lid, c.1910–20; right: cylindrical cream pot, c.1900–30. Broken items have no value.

Left: ginger beer bottle from the former Conservative Party leader William Hague's great grandfather's legacy, a Yorkshire pop company; several hundred of these were found, c.1900–20, **£8–10/$12–15**; right: Handyside's Consumption cure, black glass bottle, dug from a site now covered by a modern sports centre, c.1880–90, **£150–200/$225–300**.

landowners is not always straightforward, and you will need to persuade him/her of your good intentions to leave the site in a good state afterwards, possibly even spreading grass seed! Don't miss out third party insurance liability, and a signature removing all obligations of responsibility from the landowner.

Safety

People have been killed digging for bottles, especially when tunnelling a long way under banking. The earth can be unstable and cave in unexpectedly. Never dig alone and never tunnel dangerously. Clothing should be suited to the rigours of dump digging. Wear sturdy gloves to help avoid cuts from broken pottery and glass, and strong boots to protect the feet. Overalls are the best outer clothing for the laborious task ahead, though they are uncomfortable in hot weather, when insect repellant may prove a good idea. Bottle and jar content smells have generally long since disappeared from containers, but there can be other dangers lurking. Metal objects can easily impale, warranting a tetanus injection.

So, armed with fork and spade, off you go and have fun! Cut back the turf carefully for easy relaying after the hole has been refilled. Remove the top layer of soil and place it onto a tarpaulin or large plastic sheet, if tidiness is of the essence. An area 3 x 3m (10 x 10ft) square may be suitable; the depth of sites can vary from a foot to considerably deeper. Eventually the "seam" will be found, where all the rubbish has accumulated. Over a period of time the objects move into a compacted layer; and how to discover this will be learnt with experience. Take a bag to put the items in for carrying home, and some newspaper for any special or delicate finds.

Allowing objects to reach "room temperature" by leaving them for a day or so before attempting to clean them is wise. Many a good find has been cracked by immersing it in hot water too quickly. Hot soapy water should not harm high-fired pottery or glass and scouring with a nylon-based pad is a safe bet. However, dolls' heads should be treated very cautiously and must never be scrubbed.

A sand and water mix can help remove stubborn internal bottle stains, or seek out babies' feeding bottle brushes. Better still, visit a bottle show and you may find a range of different-sized bottle brushes, even specialist cleaning materials, and good strong gloves.

Breweriana

Young British males seem traditionally to have been quick to spend their weekly wages in the pub. Not surprising, then, that adults have developed a passion for evocative, pub-related items from their youth.

Brewery collectables from the Victorian period to the 1960s (and later) now find ready places among extensive collections worldwide. Early coaching houses, located between major conurbations, contrasted strongly with the rough and ready "spit and sawdust" public houses of the early Victorian period. All a far cry from today's family-friendly establishments.

The multitude of back bar, wall-hung, and table-top "disposables" produced over many decades are now avidly chased.

Left and right: giant labelled display bottles, c.1920–40, **£100–120/$150–180**; centre: ordinary one pint bottle, c.1930–50, **£2–3/$3–4.50**

◀ **Beer bottles**
From late Victorian times until the early 1950s, the traditional dark glass beer bottle was served from behind the bar, or carried home. These bottles were practical, they kept the contents cool, and were effectively returned intact with their vulcanite stoppers.

The internal screw stopper was invented in 1871, followed by many patent variations including Riley's "chisel head" of 1885. In 1892 the "crown cork" ousted the traditional closure, bringing the throwaway age one step nearer.

▼ **Double Diamond man**
This classic Carltonware pottery jug reflects the almost cartoon-like style of the post-war generation. Brightly coloured and suave, this upwardly-mobile middle class city gent steps forward with freshness and vitality, taking home a bottle of DD. The tightly-fitting hat is intact; without it the price is at least halved.

Double Diamond Carltonware jug, 1950s–60s, **£120–150/ $180–225**

A DOUBLE DIAMOND works wonders

GUINNESS
for strength

Both c.1950s–60s. Above:
laminated showcard, **£100–200/
$150–300**; above right:
Carltonware toucan lamp and
shade, **£500–600/$750–900**

▲ **Carltonware toucan lamp
and shade, and showcard**
Carltonware ceramic items
from the late 1950s–60s are
among the most popular of
the Breweriana fields. Mint
examples are very rare.
"Guinntiques" form a
strong collecting field
in their own
right. Later items,
such as glasses
and bottles, have
less following than
the classic Gilroy
animal designs.
Beware of
reproductions.

▼ **Beer cans**
Just before World War II,
these Brasso lookalike
beer cans were
introduced. Despite
cessation of production
during the war, these three-
piece soldered cans were not
too well received, and after
1945 were replaced with the
traditional glass bottles. Now
early beer cans are very rare.

Farrimonds FB & Mews beer
cans, 1940s, **£40–50/
$60–75**

Caley's matchstriker, 1905,
£120–150/$180–225

▲ **Caley's matchstriker**
Difficult to imagine making
an object so pretty for such a
practical purpose? Pottery
matchstrikers promoted
products on sale in the British
pub. Styles and colouring were
all part of the *raison d'être* to
attract attention and increase
sales years before television
adverts came along. The
mineral water company
Caley's displayed with pride
their Royal Patronage on the
ends of this elegant design.

Black glass

In the early years of the 17thC, wine bottles were scarce and expensive. It was not until the Victorian period and the Industrial Revolution that containers in both glass and pottery were mass-produced. This field of collecting primarily covers the period from 1650 to 1800, and in the main focuses upon wine, the staple product enjoyed by the rich.

In 1650 two-thirds of Britain was forest, but glass production was voracious in its consumption of wood to fuel the early glass houses. Coal-fired furnaces proved the saviour of what forests remained.

The term "black glass" relates to early darkly coloured bottles which have a hint of green or brown when held up to the light.

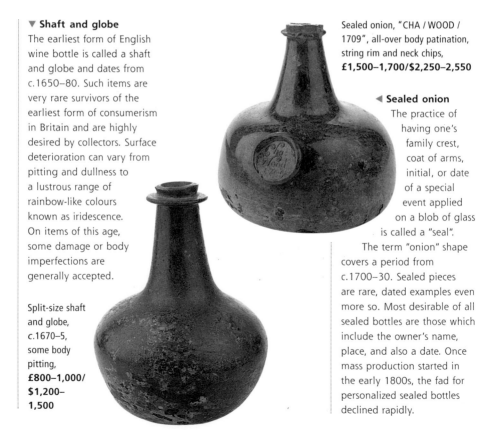

▼ Shaft and globe
The earliest form of English wine bottle is called a shaft and globe and dates from c.1650–80. Such items are very rare survivors of the earliest form of consumerism in Britain and are highly desired by collectors. Surface deterioration can vary from pitting and dullness to a lustrous range of rainbow-like colours known as iridescence. On items of this age, some damage or body imperfections are generally accepted.

Split-size shaft and globe, c.1670–5, some body pitting, **£800–1,000/ $1,200– 1,500**

Sealed onion, "CHA / WOOD / 1709", all-over body patination, string rim and neck chips, **£1,500–1,700/$2,250–2,550**

◄ Sealed onion
The practice of having one's family crest, coat of arms, initial, or date of a special event applied on a blob of glass is called a "seal".

The term "onion" shape covers a period from c.1700–30. Sealed pieces are rare, dated examples even more so. Most desirable of all sealed bottles are those which include the owner's name, place, and also a date. Once mass production started in the early 1800s, the fad for personalized sealed bottles declined rapidly.

- When viewing an auction be careful not to knock the base of one bottle against the lip or shoulder of another item; early black glass is extremely brittle.
- Dutch-made unsealed onions are lighter in colour and not as desirable as English ones.

▶ Unusual shapes

By 1695, just short of 40 bottle houses reportedly had a total annual output of over two million bottles. By 1725, Bristol had as many as 15 glass houses. Manufacturers gained recognition with distinctive and different shapes. The octagonal wine bottle shown here is extremely rare, while the very small flattened octagonal, of a much denser glass, was most possibly used by a pharmacist. Unusual forms are highly sought after and are no longer the poor cousins to their sealed counterparts.

Left: Split-size Alloa style bottle with four applied rigaree strips, c.1820–30, **£500–600/ $750–900**; right: possibly unique preserve jar, probably Nailsea, c.1830–40, **00–500/$600–750**

Left: octagonal wine bottle, c.1730–40, **£300–500/ $450–750**; right: utility bottle, c.1820–30, **£200–250/$300–375**

◀ Unusual decoration

In the mid-1800s, invention and innovation were rife. Alloa utilized strips of applied glass called "rigaree", often combined with enamelled flecks on the main body. The bottle shown here is a distinctive decanter shape. Nailsea also gained a reputation for making a variety of utilitarian forms, marked with white enamel splashing, as seen here on this preserve jar.

▼ Gins

The tapering case gin was a unique design success, shaped to fit tightly into the square compartments of wooden crates, thus facilitating more cubic capacity in the bottles. Free-blown examples from the late 1700s exist, though most found are Victorian. Pictorial examples are scarce; sealed ones even more so. The most common have two or three lines of embossed lettering.

The "PHILANTHROP" pictorial embossed case gin, c.1880–1900, **£120–150/$180–225**

Dairy items

Memories of a predominantly agriculture-based rural economy – with dairy maids in frilly hats, fresh milk ladled from the pail, and traditional farmhouse food – are part of a long-forgotten lifestyle which many may wish to imagine is still with us.

The world is a rapidly changing place, no more so than in the food and lifestyles now adopted. Objects from the past help us to learn a great deal and the lure of nostalgia should not be underestimated.

"Dairyana" covers a multitude of products: butter crocks, cream pots, milk bottles, and all the supporting promotional wares, though we should not forget the larger items such as delivery carts, milk churns, and shop cabinets, even though a little beyond the scope of this book.

Transferred two-tone MacSymons butter crock with pottery lid, c.1880–1920, **£100–120/ $150–180**

▼ MacSymons butter crock
Hand-thrown pottery butter crocks, with snugly fitting lids, were once to be found in all large, well-to-do households and hotels. Transfer-printed examples such as this MacSymons Stores crock tells us their shops were located in more than one town, in this case Liverpool and Greenock, Scotland. Sometimes such crocks have two small side handles and range from 450g (1lb) up to a massive 9kg (20lb) catering size. The original lid is normally absent.

▲ Cream pots
Coloured-top pictorial cream pots such as the Buttercup Cream pot are avidly collected. The cream pot range also includes "cylinders" (see above centre). A tiny handle is often incorporated as in this distinctive churn shape from the Helsby Creamery.

All c.1900–30. Left to right: blue transferred Buttercup Cream, **£25–30/ $40–45**; Horner's red-print cylinder, **£30–40/ $45–60**; Helsby, **£15–20/$25–30**

Left: wide-necked third of a pint milk bottle, c.1940s, **£7–10/$10–15**; centre: cardboard disc closure, c.1940s, **£1–2/$3**; right: advertising bottle, 1960s, **£3–5/$5–8**

▲ Milk bottles
Wide-necked milk bottles, mostly from between the war years, featured a pull-out card disc closure and "pyro" transfer. This red-print third of a pint (see *above left*) was produced for school use. Local place names add regional appeal. In the late 1960s/early 1970s, a big push was made to save the home-delivered glass "pinta" by advertising various products on the sides. It caught on in a big way, providing us today with a wide range of low-cost collectables.

▼ Andrew Cameron, Ayr
Stoneware transfer-printed cream pots generally cost £10–50/$15–75, with a large assortment to choose from. However, as with all areas of collecting, rarities command high values, especially ones with coloured tops in blue or green, and coloured transfers, or a combination of both. This blue transfer-printed "Andrew Cameron / Provision Merchant / Ayr", with large cow pictorial, is among the best-struck examples of only a handful so far found. Indeed, most of the others feature quite poor transfers. Scotland, especially in the southwest, produced a good number of different pots.

Blue transfer-printed Andrew Cameron, c.1920s, **£800–1,000/ $1,200–1,500**

Farm scene, E. Bannister, Sheffield, c.1900–20, **£25–30/$35–45**

▲ E. Bannister, Sheffield
Cream pot designs range from simple lettering to some fairly detailed pictorial transfers, usually depicting cows. This E. Bannister pot, one of three sizes known, presents a tranquil image of cows, fields, farmhouse, and dairy maid. The same pot is also found with a Huddersfield address.

Doulton

The world-renowned pottery company Royal Doulton stems from humble beginnings on the banks of London's River Thames in the 1820s. John Doulton and John Watts produced flasks, tankards, and pitkins for the drinks trade, and all manner of essential utilitarian wares from candlesticks to large storage containers. Mass production of such a vast range of goods, now regularly dump-dug by 21st-century collectors, links the Doulton name inextricably with the modern bottle fraternity. Dump diggers worldwide are familiar with the boot-blacking jars, bulk inks, ginger beers, whisky jugs, and spirit flasks all bearing the "Doulton & Watts, Lambeth" impressed mark. Today's collectors are magnetically drawn to this name.

Sample miniature flagon, 1890–1900s, **£120–150/$180–225**, (without original stopper **£60–70/$90–105**)

▶ **Sample flagon**
This miniature flagon, complete with internal screw stopper, clearly promotes the multitude of areas Doulton supplied. It reads "Doulton / Lambeth / Bottles for / Brewers & / Distillers / Made Specially / Strong By / Patent Process." It was possibly given away to brewers to coax additional sales of their pottery.

▼ **Cleaning fluid bottle**
It is difficult to imagine the great need for certain past products, such as this quite rare survivor of the Edwardian age. Fox hunting was once a popular pastime in Britain; on winter days the hunt and hounds would gather for a quick "tot" outside the village pub before the hunt commenced. Hunts were social gatherings and the huntsmen needed to appear well groomed. Hence the need for "Stohwasser & Winters / Gloire D'Eclaire ...", cleaning fluid for hunting coats.

Cleaning fluid bottle, c.1920s, **£40–50/$60–75**

▼ Stamp damper

David Lloyd George was a famed orator, so using his wide-open mouth was an appropriate choice for a stamp damper. It was sold with a sponge "tongue" concealing the filling hole, providing the user with a moist surface on which to "damp" stamps. This item commemorated the introduction of the National Insurance Act of 1914, a social revolution championed by Lloyd George, which took four pence per week from all workers in return for medical and financial benefits during sickness.

Lloyd George stamp damper, c.1914, **£200–250/$300–375**

Doulton Lambeth artware soft drinks dispenser, c.1880–1900, **£500–700/$750–1,000**

▲ Soft drinks dispenser

Imagine a London gentleman's club in 1885, where city gents retired for a late afternoon discussion, cigar, and a brandy. In the early evening their wives, often with young children, would call to collect them in chauffeur-driven motor cars. As only men were allowed into the club, a gentleman's family would announce their arrival and await his emergence, the children partaking of free, iced, orange squash from the magnificent Doulton artware dispenser on the corner shelf.

▼ Dulux dog

Many companies utilized the Doulton Lambeth and Burslem factories for the manufacture of promotional materials. The large Dulux dog, made by Beswick, a company taken over by Doulton in the 1930s, is a 1960s "icon"; an advertising image embedded in Britain's social heritage. The exact number made for shop window display purposes is unknown.

Dulux dog, c.1964–70, **£300–350/ $450–525**

Fire grenades

From the 1870s mould-made glass fire grenades (so called because they were used much like military hand-thrown grenades) could be purchased in both Britain and America. They were found in hotels, railway carriages, factories, schools, and homes as singles or in racks of two, three, or more. Available in a variety of colours and shapes with embossed raised patterns, they contained ingredients such as water, carbolic acid, chalk, and sulphur. With the invention of the telephone to summon a fire engine with a plentiful supply of water, such devices rapidly disappeared. Today they are rare and avidly collected for their rich and varied colours.

▼ **Promotional ephemera**
Most companies provided promotional material, from self-acclaiming fliers to quite substantial almanacs with subtle testimonials and proclamations. All fire grenade related ephemera is scarce, but it often contains enormously valuable background information for the collector. This example illustrates six different racks for holding from one to six grenades, along with purchase price. Note the grenade's price of £345 per dozen.

Imperial fire extinguisher 4-page leaflet, c.1887, **£30–40/ $45–60**

▲ **Rack of grenades**
Grenades could be purchased in various rack styles for wall mounting, or elegant hall stands to suit a stylish Victorian/Edwardian home amidst aspidistras and velvet curtains! Complete racks are now extremely rare. When found, they often have the original wire round the neck to hold each grenade in place – probably cumbersome to undo. This rack of three was found intact in a Channel Island barn.

Hardens rack of three cobalt blue "Star" grenades, c.1880–1900, **£200–250/ $300–450**

Kalamazoo cobalt blue
grenade, c.1880–1900,
£250–300/$375–450

▲ **Kalamazoo grenade**
Fire grenade designs generally
have a long neck to facilitate
easy handling. The Kalamazoo,
a distinctively unique
American design, is found
in deep cobalt blue, perfectly
displaying the need for the
form to suit its function.
It is embossed "The
Kalamazoo Automatic and
Hand Fire Extinguisher /
Patent Applied For". The
latter means that an
application for patent
protection was made, though
often full granting not given.

▼ **Système Labbe, Paris**
Apart from Britain and
America, France is a good
hunting ground for a variety
of different grenade designs.
This empty golden amber
example is strikingly patterned
with ribs to the lower section,
diamonds in two circles, and
texturing to the top half.
　　It is often found complete
with a test tube-like neck
hanging device providing
a mix of water and carbon
tetrachlorides. According
to claims, it doused the fire
more effectively than water.

Système Labbe amber
glass grenade, c.1900–20,
£100–150/$150–225

Pint green "Hardens Star"
grenade, c.1884,
£300–400/$450–600

▲ **Green "Hardens Star"**
This famous model was first
patented in 1871 in America.
In a vibrant apple green
colour, this rare pint size
example is embossed on the
base "May 27 '84" and on
the body with a prominent
raised star and the word "star"
within a circle. The rest of the
body is fluted.

Ginger beer

During the Industrial Revolution there was a growing demand in rapidly expanding towns and cities for a cheap, casual thirst quencher. Ginger beer was just the right drink, necessitating no complex machinery. From early Victorian times to the 1950s, a ginger beer plant was not uncommon in many working-class households. The drink was traditionally packaged in cool stoneware bottles, hence the term "stone ginger". In 1928, Mary Donoghue sued a ginger beer maker after finding a decomposed snail shell in her bottle, effectively sealing the fate of such receptacles. Today's collectors inherit a rich legacy of "g.b.s" (as they are affectionately known) of various shapes, some with coloured tops or pictorial transfers.

Left: standard g.b., c.1900–20, **£15–20/$20–30**; right: bulk dispenser, c.1900–20, very rare, **£120–150/$180–225**

▶ **The Ludford Ginger**
Trademarks often reflect what in the past was a key aspect of a town or region such as on these bottles from Crewe, once a world-renowned and important railway hub, and train building centre. The rare 8 pt (1 gal) bulk dispenser complete with internal screw pottery stopper, and metal carrying handle, incorporates the same distinctive train trademark.

▼ **Skittle shape**
The term "skittle" reflects a particular style similar to the pin used in the bowling game. Few companies adopted this distinctive shape. The rare split-size example (see left) features the later crown cork top (invented in 1892) and provided only a small amount of thirst-quenching liquid. The normal-sized bottle (see right) has an unusual tan colour body with a black overglazed transfer of poor quality.

Left: split size "Bewick Brothers/ Edinburgh", c.1900–20, **£50–80/ $75–120**; right: "Thomson's / Aberdeen", c.1900–20, **£40–50/$60–75**

st = standard – straight sides, short angled shoulder.

ch = champagne – straight sides but gently sloping long neck.

tt = two-tone – top one colour (usually tan/brown), lower part off-white/cream.

cc = crown cap.

▼ R. Emmerson Junr.

The R. Emmerson man on a penny farthing pictorial is a classic and highly-regarded Buchan pottery-made champagne-shape "stonie". Northeast England is an area rich in quality pictorial gingers. Because a good number have been dug in recent years, they currently remain quite affordable. Illustrated below is the much rarer variant marked "The Doctors Stout / Ross & Co" carrying the same pictorial trademark.

R. Emmerson Junr., The Doctors Stout, c.1900–20, **£30–35/$45–52.50**

Joseph Gidman Galtee More patent, Knutsford, Cheshire, c.1900–20, rare, **£50–60/$75–90**

▲ Galtee More patent

Wiring on a cork, banged tightly into the neck, was a fiddly process. The 1897 Galtee More patent attempted, unsuccessfully, to overcome this with the provision of a small hole in the side of the blob top through which a metal pin could be inserted.
It had a short period of popularity after its invention, and only a handful of companies appear to have used it.

▼ Lawrance & Sons

The Norfolk-based Lawrance & Sons company adopted a unique reverse two-tone bottle design with a large number of minor transfer variations, including numerous town names from that region. Subtle transfer variations can make a great difference between what is common and what is rare, and bring a big price differential.

Lawrance & Sons, Yarmouth & Stalham, a common variation from this company, c.1900–20, **£10–15/$15–25**

▼ Miniature g.b.s

It is uncertain just why miniature g.b.s were made, or indeed how. Pure promotional purposes may be the reason. All are now rare. They range in size from 3.5cm (1¼in) Doulton (the smallest) saltglaze examples up to the largest, a 19cm (7¾in) bottle promoting Fulham Pottery. Distinctly different in nature are full-size bottles advertising different pottery companies (see *opposite*). Both miniatures shown here are two-tone examples.

Left: Robinson & Co., Hull, 5.5cm (2¼in) tall, c.1920, **£60–80/$90–120**; right: Dartnel's ginger beer, c.1920, **£50–70/$75–110**

Redruth Brewery Co., Redruth, c.1900–20, **£10–20/$15–30**

▲ Redruth Brewery Co.

A man in a wicker basket, holding a bottle in one hand and feeding the man in the moon with the other, while being held aloft by a giant bird, is itself a remarkable pictorial trademark concept. However, such strange images clearly epitomize the inventiveness of the later Victorian/early Edwardian period and may even relate to a well-known incident of the time, now long since forgotten. This all tan-coloured standard-shape ginger comes from southwest England, not overly famed for good pictorial examples.

▼ Pictorial variations

These two ginger beers differ distinctly in colour and shape, though both are referred to as "standard" type. A large number of the Comrie & Co., Helensburgh bottles were found in the 1980s but few were in mint condition or featured a sharp transfer. The price of these two pieces reflects both being in an excellent state. Often there can be an overlap between collecting areas, and the rare saltglaze cricket bat pictorial from Rhyl, North Wales, excites both bottlers and sporting collectors.

Left: Comrie & Co., Helensburgh, c.1900–20, **£60–80/$90–120**; right: Rhyl cricket bat pictorial, 1890–1900, **£80–100/$120–150**

All c.1900–20. From left to right: Buckler & Co., Exeter, very rare, **£300–400/$450–600**; Horsham, **£40–50/$60–75**; "E. B. Storm / Worcester", very rare, **£120–150/$180–225**

▲ Coloured tops

Sometimes bottle collectors refer to "only two or three recorded". This specialist collecting field is very knowledgeable and people really do know such exact information as total numbers known to exist. A great rarity is this blue top blue transfer Buckler & Co., Exeter, southwest England. Less than five examples are recorded, and despite a base chip this remains highly desirable and sought after by local collectors and specialists of coloured-top gingers.

▶ Three unusual oddities

The first (*left*) is a 750ml (26fl oz) size champagne promotional piece from the George Skey Tamworth Pottery, dug in Australia and a presumed salesman's sample. Bottles this size are generally only found in very hot climates such as South Africa, Australia, and South America. The Stiff & Sons (*centre*) is a rare London saltglaze bottle. No Doulton promotional transferred g.b. has yet been found. Meanwhile, the Fulham Pottery piece (*right*) is a strange mid-range size, neither mini nor full, also promoting the associated Fulham Filter Co.

Left: Skey advertising ginger, c.1920, **£150–200/$225–300**; centre: Stiff & Sons, c.1900–20, **£200–250/$300–375**; right: Fulham Pottery saltglaze, c.1880–1900, **£300–400/$450–600**, (in excess of **£500/$750** with coloured lip)

Go-withs

From the late 1960s onwards, specialist bottle fairs evolved a range of extra visitor attractions, one of which was competitions. Collectors were invited to take along their favourite and prized items, presented in a visually interesting way. Competitors were encouraged to incorporate supporting materials, which were dubbed "go-withs". In effect, this refers to all manner of promotional and shop-related material: card, tin, or enamel advertisements; original cabinets; ephemera, and packaging. This is an extensive and very broad range with enormous scope in its own right, way beyond the scope of this book, but a brief selection is shown here to whet the appetite.

▼ **Shoe-shine box**
Before running shoes and trainers, everyone who could afford footwear valued handmade leather shoes. Constant care and treatment was essential to protect the shoe and prolong its life. This fuelled the need for a portable shoe-shine box, with a rear flap for carrying brushes, clothes, and some "Cherry Blossom Boot Polish".

Shoe-shine stand, 31cm (12½in) tall and 41cm (16¼in) wide, wood with enamel side panels, c.1920–40, **£300–400/ $450–600**

▶ **Advertising shop chair**
Every corner shop from the mid-Victorian period to the 1950s provided a chair for customers waiting to be served. Manufacturers seized on the opportunity of offering a chair, in exchange for promoting their products, mostly in the form of a lettered enamel back. Many were burnt in the 1960s clear-outs and are consequently prized today. Double-sided enamel backs are preferred to single-sided ones.

Advertising chair, 95cm (37½in) tall, enamelled back, c.1920–40, **£400–500/ $600–750**

- Condition can make an enormous difference to the value of an item.
- Display any printed items (tin or card) away from direct sunlight to avoid fading.
- Reproductions are common in this area of collecting. Always ask for provenance, even a note of authenticity.

▼ Chocolate display cabinet

Numerous brand names from the past have disappeared, but many chocolate makers capitalized on children's sweet teeth by temptingly presenting sweets in glass shop display cabinets. This proved enormously effective. Chocolate is a very strong collecting area, and old advertising cabinets are now in high demand.

Fry's cabinet, 48cm (19½in) to pediment top, c.1920–40, **£500–1,000/$750–1,500**

Pressed "Players" tin sign, 30cm (12in) diam., good condition, c.1920–40, **£350–400/$525–600**, (generally worn and/or rusted, **£150–200/$225–300**)

▲ Player's Navy Mixture sign

Pressed tin signs proved to be far more durable than card, but less costly than enamel signs. These were at the height of their popularity between the World Wars, and the bearded "Players Please" sailor became a familiar trademark worldwide. The surface of such signs, however, is easily scratched, and collectors should be careful when transporting them. Wrap in tissue or plastic, and take care not to bend corners. Consequently, examples in mint condition command a premium.

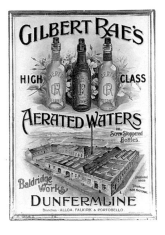

Gilbert Rae's pressed tin sign, 50 x 72cm (20 x 28in), c.1890–1910, **£400–600/$600–900**

▲ Mineral water advertisement

Promotional material for mineral waters is scarce, and keenly contested whenever it appears for sale. Sometimes old showcards are found behind framed prints, or family photographs. This sign is one of a handful uncovered in the derelict remains of the original pop factory in Dunfermline, Scotland.

In the bathroom

Towards the end of the Victorian era, a combination of factors, spearheaded by the Industrial Revolution, led to an explosion of terraced houses in towns and cities, many for the first time offering a flushing lavatory and fitted bath. A diverse and broad range of small collectable items can be found with a bathroom, or bedroom, connection. Here is but a small offering. Footwarmers, for example, can be found in many styles, running into hundreds!

"Lootiques" covers an even more specialized area of any item connected with the toilet. Related advertising for various cleaning products, soaps (Pears offers a vast range), and lotions expands the scope even further.

Razobrite Bath complete with razor and pack of blades, c.1920–40, **£40–50/$60–75**

▼ Lavatory disinfectors
Another simple but effective concept, whereby a stoneware container was filled with disinfectant and placed in the cistern. Flushing activated the dispersal of a small amount of disinfectant through a glass or pottery tube (see *below right*). The containers were returned to the local hardware store for refilling: a very environmentally-friendly idea. A few different examples can be found, though generally some damage is expected.

▲ Razobrite Bath
An ingenious combination of a ceramic base and lid designed to discreetly hold a gentleman's razor, with the handle protruding through a hole in the top. A neat and tidy all-in-one invention from America, made the more collectable by having a vivid blue glazed top.

Left: Taylors Rolyat Disinfector (minus glass tube), c.1900–20, **£30–40/$45–60**; right: Maw's Lavatory Disinfector, c.1900–20, **£30–40/$45–60**

Teddy bear hot-water bottle, (cost 1/11d when new) c.1920–30, **£300–400/$450–600**

▲ Teddy bear hot-water bottle

Before 20thC central heating, the living-room fire was often the only source of warmth. Bedtime in winter was uncomfortably cold. Large pebbles, heated in the oven, were wrapped in cloth and put in the bed. Stoneware hot water bottles towards the end of the Victorian period became an essential item. Elaborate figurals (fish, rabbits, bears, etc) by Denby Pottery and Lovatt & Lovatt are rare.

▼ Transferred bedwarmers

Saltglazed "brick"-shaped bedwarmers were superceded in later Victorian years by more attractive transfer-printed types. Flat rectangular or circular shapes enabled pictorial transfers to be used. The Bungalow Footwarmer from the 1920s to 1930s echoed the modern in-vogue housing style, whilst the small Adaptable example "... for muff or pocket" warmed people sitting in the back of a horsedrawn coach, landau, or motor car. Examples featuring the name of the manufacturer are highly desirable.

Left: Bungalow Footwarmer, c.1920–30, **£70–100/ $100–150**; right: Adaptable muff warmer, c.1890–1920, **£80–120/$120–180**

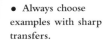
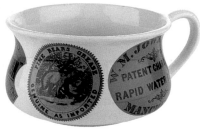

Coloured Portmeirion potty, c.1962–70, **£30–40/$45–60**

▲ Portmeirion pottery

Original copperplate images rescued from Kirkham Pottery's attic in 1962 were used on a surprisingly extensive range of mugs, jars, plates, and potties (see above). While not quite the original old items this book covers, they do fit nicely into the bathroom/kitchen theme.

Indeed, they may be a good future investment; currently affordable, but destined to rise. Look out for them at carboot sales. Most are just black and white.

Pottery inks

Several factors led to the production of a huge and fascinating range of pottery or glass containers to store ink. In Britain, from 1840 the penny post simplified the task of sending mail. By 1842, Joseph Gillott (pen manufacturer to Queen Victoria) was making 70 million steel nibbed pens per year. Pottery companies soon directed their ideas to ingenious, unusual, and sometimes highly decorative ink bottles. In the early 1800s they were made in the traditional, brown saltglaze finish, but as competition increased with the glass manufacturers towards the turn of the century, Doulton artwares, and coloured and transfer-printed examples emerged.

Today, ink bottles and inkwells form one of the most popular specialist bottle collecting areas, and are appreciated worldwide.

▼ **Penny pot**
The simplest and cheapest saltglaze stoneware ink was the "penny pot", so-called because it cost 1d per pot. These were hand thrown on a potter's wheel, one at a time, from a large lump of clay. The makers were paid on a piece rate, and making such small items led to arthritis of the hands in later life.

This impressed "1-V Perfume Ink" is an uncommon example and intended for writing love letters.

Farrars perfumed ink, c.1880–1900, **£30–40/ $45–60**

▶ **Bulk ink**
Late Victorian school desks sported small ceramic inkwells, refilled by ink monitors. One gallon jars down to more amenable, pint size, bulk bottles like this paper-labelled example were used in both schools and offices. Ink came in red, blue, or black. Unfortunately drips often spoil the label, therefore the cleaner the label the higher the price. Beware of reproduced labels.

"Swan Red Ink" labelled bulk bottle, c.1930–50, **£15–20/ $20–30**

▼ Harwood's desk ink

An essential aspect for effective ink bottle design is one which does not spill easily, and an added bonus is for the pen to be held in the well. This early 1830s piece performs both. The name of the retailer, "Harwood's / Superior Black Writing Ink / 26 Fenchurch St / London" is impressed clearly across the top. Lead shot was often put inside the bottle to clean the nib during use.

Dark brown saltglazed Harwood's desk ink, c.1830–40, **£170–200/$225–300**

Virago "Votes for Women" inkwell, Doulton, c.1907–18, **£300–350/$450–525**

▲ Virago inkwell

Emily Pankhurst and the women's suffragette movement were, tongue in cheek, represented by the Doulton Lambeth made stoneware inkwell. It is hinged behind the head and usually impressed across the apron "Votes for Women". They were produced from 1907 to 1918, although the pattern number, 7235, was not accepted until 1909. There are more than ten minor colour and design variations, plus a saltglaze baby version, though naturally not a male one!

▼ Ma & Pa Carter

To monitor the power of advertising, American magazines, c.1914, carried adverts with coupons to be mailed back with twenty-five cents for a pair of inkwells. The advert proved hugely successful, with 50,000 returned. Thanks to Carter Ink Co. of Boston, Massachusetts, for thus instigating the junk mail of today! The wells are difficult to obtain despite large numbers made.

Ma & Pa Carter, c.1914, **£120–150/$180–225**

Glass inks

With the onslaught of the Industrial Revolution, and a growing market economy, came the ability to mass-produce. This was illustrated nowhere better than in the glass industry. Millions of bottles were produced very cheaply. Ink manufacturers capitalized on glass in a big way, judging by the discovery of so many basic shapes: square, rectangular, some ribbed and some not, and some with a recess for a free nib.

Most bottles are aqua green with a jagged "sheared lip" finish to bite deeply into the cork before sealing with wax, and are crude and full of tiny air bubbles. Some novel shapes also appeared to compete with the fancier pottery forms. Most of these are now rare and highly desirable.

Left to right: aqua square ribbed & dark aqua octagonal, c.1890–1920, **£3–4/$5–6** (each); blue "boat", c.1890–1910, **£12–15/$18–20**

▲ **Common sheared lips**
There are many of the commoner sheared lip forms available and they are a relatively good buy, considering their age. Cobalt blue examples are highly desirable, but amber are actually the rarest.

▼ **Labelled tipper**
A simple but ingenious development of the plain sheared lip design is the "tipper", intending to recover the very last drop of ink from the bottom of the bottle. These appear most often in the Lincolnshire area, in the Midlands, suggesting a regional connection of some kind, as yet unproven. There are three variations, the octagonal one seen here, a longer octagonal, and a circular tipper. No coloured examples have, as yet, surfaced. This is a scarce labelled example, complete with most of the original red ink.

Labelled octagonal tipper, c.1920–30, **£30–40/$45–60**, (unlabelled, **£3–5/ $4–8**)

▼ Cottage ink

Attempting to lure customers into purchasing a glass container, as opposed to a pottery one, was not always simply a case of providing the cheapest. Novelty designs were devised, the glass cottage being now the most famous and desirable. Overall embossing of roof, windows, and water butt can vary. Some display a rear recess for a nib; this particularly rare example features a diamond registration mark. There is also a cottage shape without any embossing or decoration, believed to be a little later.

Aqua cottage ink, c.1880–1900, **£300–400/$450–600**, (without diamond registration, **£80–120/ $120–180**)

Amber "Field's Ink & Gum" bottle, c.1915–30, **£30–40/$45–60**, (aqua example, **£2–3/$3–5**)

▲ Field's Ink & Gum

Very few glass ink bottles feature embossed lettering across the front, most used a paper label. This square Field's bottle contained either ink or gum, the registered number 660694 indicating it was first made c.1915–16 but made up to the 1930s. Digging Edwardian dumps has become necessary as Victorian sites have dried up, but items such as this can make the toil well worthwhile.

▼ Teakettles

Professionals required a glass ink receptacle of greater refinement than the rudimentary plain aqua sheared lips, for their leather-topped wooden desks. The so-called "teakettle" design fulfilled this criteron perfectly. It was made in a multitude of glass colours, and pottery, and originally mounted in gilt frames, most of which have long since gone. They are now all rare and keenly sought.

Left to right: amber glass teakettle, c.1830–60, **£300–350/ $450–525**; pottery teakettle, c.1830–60, **£250–300/$375–450**; embossed green glass teakettle, c.1840–60, **£400–500/ $600–750**

Kitchenalia

Before microwaves, food mixers and blenders, the kitchen represented a world of toil for the cook. Large families and low incomes dictated food and drink were almost exclusively home-made in Victorian times. Pottery and glass containers came into their own in the kitchen, as they were ideal for keeping their contents cool. Transfers and paper labels covered a multitude of ingenious shapes designed for holding everything from soup to meat extract. This collecting category is rich in novelty and attractive items, spreading across the Victorian period and up to World War II. Kitchenalia, including gadgets and related advertising, affords massive scope for adding period detail to a modern fitted kitchen.

▼ Sauce bottles

Most sauce bottles tend to be made of quite plain aqua glass, and are not collected. However, there are exceptions worth seeking out, especially bottles for elaborate pepper sauces. Shown here is an unusual amber glass Fletcher's Tiger Sauce bottle. Alongside it is an HP Sauce bottle, a best-seller with its label depicting the Houses of Parliament. This example is complete with its stopper.

Left: amber glass, Tiger Sauce, c.1920–30, **£15–20/ $20–30**; right: HP Sauce, c.1930–40, **£10–15/$15–20**

▶ Rock Blue

Scotland's Buchan pottery made a number of variations of this unusual laundry item, all featuring the pictorial trademark with sailing ship, rocks, and setting sun. What makes this model particularly desirable is the blue top and sometimes blue transfer, but also the charming address "W R Hatton & Sons Ltd/Wormwood Scrubs". The elaborate transfer on this bottle gives the following details: "gold medal 1896 & 3 gold medals 1896, 7 gold medals 1900"; most probably awarded at a trade fair. "Blue makers to His Majesty the King" records Royal patronage.

Rock Blue, blue transfer, c.1900, **£60–80/ $90–120**

FACT FILE

Cleaning kitchenalia
Any pottery or glass, tin or enamel displayed in the kitchen can be safely cleaned in warm soapy water using a soft cloth, not a metal pad. Original paper labels should be protected with a clear plastic film, or they will soon ruin.

Both c.1900–20. Giant labelled Bovril bottle, **£150–200/ $225–300**; standard small example, **£1–2/$2–3**

▲ Bovril
The Scotsman John Lawson Johnston developed Johnstons Fluid in Canada in 1874. A factory fire in 1884 saw him relocate to London, where he registered the name Bovril in 1887. In 1888, he introduced the now distinctive bottle shape. The giant shop display bottle is the most desirable, though others now cost from just pence up to a few pounds.

▼ Pie funnels
Bottle collecting reveals an insight into our past eating habits. In hurly-burly modern society, few of us have time to make home-made pies. The pottery pie funnel was an essential item up to 50 years ago, supporting the pastry in the middle and allowing air to escape. Over 100 variations are awaiting your discovery. Figurals shaped as elephants and blackbirds complement advertising examples similar to those shown.

Both c.1920–40. Right: "The Improved Popular Pie Funnel", **£30–40/$45–60**; left: "The Grimwade Improved Perfection Pie Funnel", **£40–60/$60–90**

"R Wotherspoon & Co" transferred two-tone jar, rare, c.1910–20, **£60–80/$90–120**

▲ Marmalade pots
In Britain bread and jam, or marmalade, was a favourite working-class snack up to the 1950s. There was little wrong with the fruit, sugar, and fresh bread diet. Transferred marmalade pots offer an affordable range for the collector on a budget; Keiller's types start from £2/$3 upwards. The original greaseproof paper tops have long since disappeared.

Mineral waters

Joseph Priestley discovered a practical method of manufacturing artificial mineral water in 1772. However, retaining the fizz in glass bottles became a long-standing problem. William Hamilton's solution in the early 1800s was a bottle with a pointed end, which was unable to stand up and therefore lay sideways keeping the cork moist and the fizz intact. Intervening decades saw masses of patents trying to threaten this American invention. Hiram Codd's marble-stoppered bottle became a world beater from the 1870s, establishing a revolutionary vast glass industry. This novel invention was expensive to manufacture, as it needed to be returned and refilled ten times for profitability. Unusual patent variations, plus an extensive range of different colours and lips, make this one of the top bottle categories.

Dark olive green pontilled embossed hamilton, 19cm (7¾in), c.1820–40, **£700–1,000/ $1,000–1,500**

▲ Hamilton's patent

Early pontil-marked embossed hamiltons are among the most desirable of mineral water bottles. This example shows signs of wear and surface patination. Some collectors see this as adding character to an object almost 200 years old. Embossed "Hamiltons Patent Aerated Waters & C / Sold by / R Johnston 15 Greek St Soho / London". Pottery hamiltons are also recorded.

▼ Flat-bottomed hamiltons

There is no logic to the hamilton bottle requiring a pointed end. For years, wine bottles were stored on their sides to keep corks moist. Maybe once the cork was removed, and the bottle was unable to be laid down, usage and consequently sales increased. As the 1900s drew to a close and the marble-stoppered codd bottle lost popularity, the flat-bottomed hamilton was introduced in an attempt to increase the lifespan of a patent. This mid-blue example features a pictorial stag's head trademark. Blue glass was an exceptional novelty for "pop".

Mid-blue, flat-bottomed hamilton, 18.5cm (7½in), c.1900–20, **£200–250/$300–375**, (dark blue example, **£400–500/$600–750**)

"Geo. Taylor / Sheffield / 1893",
aqua glass valve patent codd,
19cm (7¾in), c.1893,
£120–150/$180–225

▼ Codd hamilton hybrid

Hiram Codd's famous marble closure was patented on September 3rd 1872. It was filled on a machine which simultaneously spun the bottle through 180 degrees, during which it injected a small amount of gas, pressing the marble firmly against the top of the rubber washer in the neck. William Hamilton's point-ended design was combined with the marble closure to produce the codd hamilton hybrid, retaining customers loyal to both shapes. Rare examples feature coloured lips.

Aqua codd hamilton hybrid with amber marble, 18.5cm (7½in), c.1900, **£120–150/$180–225**, (example with aqua marble, **£30–50/$45–75**)

▲ Valve codd

Imagine Frances Hodgson Burnett's Little Lord Fauntleroy pressing down the marble on a codd bottle and accidentally spurting cherryade all over his suit…. The 1882 "Crystal" patent introduced a cunning valve device into the neck – a glass valve held in by a rubber washer which overcame all of the problems encountered with previous devices by simply pressing it in, releasing the pressure, and allowing the marble to drop. As it was costly to manufacture it was used by only a few of companies, making it scarce today.

▼ Coloured lip codds

In 1889, Dan Ryland's sales catalogue promoted codds with coloured lips in blue, green, or brown to avoid competitors reusing another company's empties. Only one lip colour per town, naturally. This blue-lipped Reliance patent was exported to South Africa from the Rylands Stairfoot Factory, Barnsley, northeast England. The dark brown-lipped Reliance features coloured swirls in the body.

Left: blue lip Reliance patent, 1892, **£150–200/$225–300**; right: dark brown lip, Reliance patent, only example recorded "P.B.N.", c.1890–1900, **£2,000–3,000/$3,000–4,500**

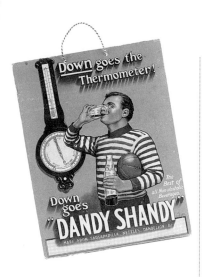

Dandy Shandy card advert,
30 x 23cm (12 x 9in), c.1900–20,
£30–50/$45–75

▲ Dandy Shandy advert

Pictorial mineral water
advertisements to accompany
the bottles are generally rare,
and thus expensive. One
which is affordable is the
Dandy Shandy card advert,
found in both a summer
version ("Up goes the
thermometer") featuring
a man in a straw boater,
and a winter version shown
here ("Down goes the
thermometer"). A number
were discovered in the back of
an old print store several years
ago, and they re-appear from
time to time in the most
unlikely of places.

▼ Pontilled codd

Collectors of bottles must rate
among the most intense and
knowledgeable of any
collecting field. Claims of
"the only example recorded"
are genuinely based upon
a well-oiled bush telegraph
information superhighway.
A rare discovery in one area is
news worldwide the next day.
A chance discovery a few years
ago, during construction of a
house, was this pontilled codd
bottle. It remains the world's
only example, with no
explanation or reason as to
why such a bottle was made.

A Barnsley-made pontilled amber
codd, bearing no mineral water
company name, c.1880,
£2,000–3,000/$3,000–4,500

Barrett & Elers wooden plug
patent, aqua glass, c.1870–80,
£20–30/$30–45

▲ Barrett & Elers
wooden plug

The first major internal stopper
specification in the trade was
Adams & Barrett's patent in
1868. Barrett & Elers perfected
the more widely adopted
wooden plug device a few
years later. No longer was
there a need to fiddle with
corks in hamiltons. Sealing
and opening the fizzy drink
suddenly became a relatively
simple operation. The prospect
of splinters in the tongue from
long-term refilling and re-use
does not bear thinking about!

▼ Amber Keystone codd

To increase sales, mineral water manufacturers took on a plethora of developments dreamt up by the glass companies. From 1880 to the turn of the century, fine-tuned subtle patent specifications were in abundance. Only two mineral firms in the world, one in Birmingham and the other in Sheffield, adopted a coloured codd bottle with a subtle multi-faceted base as their particular and unique style.

Amber-faceted base Keystone Steam Bottling Company codd, Birmingham, 10oz capacity, c.1880–1900,
£150–200/$225–300

Cobalt Goffe & Sons, Birmingham, bulb neck codd, 17cm (6¾in) tall, c.1880–90,
£2,000–3,000/$3,000–4,500

▲ Cobalt Goffe & Sons bulb-neck codd

It seemed an extraordinary concept over a hundred years ago to package a fizzy drink in a deep blue glass bottle, particularly when this colour was often used to warn away unsuspecting consumers of toxic substances in poison bottles. This vibrant packaging colour was most commonly found in northeast England. Today, Goffe & Sons' deep blue glass bulb neck codd rates as one of the most desirable of its type.

▼ Green codds

Most codd bottles bore embossed lettering, a paper side label, and some had a small base label. Green glass came in a variety of shades, the one on the left referred to as emerald, and on the right as olive green. A mixed grouping of good condition, coloured and coloured-lip mineral waters, when backlit, is an impressive sight, even to non-initiated onlookers.

Both c.1890–1900. Left: emerald green codd, 6oz, **£80–120/ $120–180**; right: olive green codd, 10oz, **£50– 70/$75–105**

Ointment pots

A large range of ceramic pots can be found which once contained ointment (a word derived from the Greek *unguent*). They are similar in size to plastic ointment containers found today in pharmacies or drug stores. Examples cover the mid to late 1700s, through late Victorian years (when quackery was at its peak) right up to Edwardian times. For less than £100/$150 you can start a collection with Singleton's Golden Eye Ointment for £2–3/$3–5; Clarke's Miraculous Salve and Egyptian Salve for £12–15/$18–20 each; Poor Man's Friend (blue transfer front and back); Holloway's Ointment (seated robed lady, with child), and Nature's Herbal Ointment for £15–20/$20–30 each. Thereafter the chase becomes more challenging, with numerous variations too.

Early delft style tin-glazed ointment pot, 6cm (2½in) tall, c.1750–1800, **£50–100/ $75–150**

▼ **Delft pot**
A simple hand-thrown tin-glazed earthenware pot without markings. Examples with much shallower bowls can be found with rudimentary hand-painted ornamentation or with simple lettering such as Waller & Son and Delescot. Decorated delft examples cost from £200/$300 to £500/$750, according to condition. Though it is generally accepted that most pieces are damaged, minor edge flakes or chips are preferable to large body cracks. Important, well-preserved pieces can easily soar over £1,000/ $1,500 in value.

▶ **Lees's Ointment**
Pictorial ointment pots, except for Holloway's, are extremely rare. This Scottish example goes one further, with a fine image of Stanley castle and supporting words encircling the pot – all in sepia. "Lees's Ointment ... Paisley" claims to cure "inveterate ulcers, sore breasts, bad legs, sore heads, foul shaves, and all skin diseases." The extreme rarity of this pot would suggest a possibly short-term business operation, unable to compete with more extensive advertising from the more successful companies.

"Lees's Ointment Paisley Sepia" three-part transfer, 6cm (2½in) tall, c.1880–1900, **£400–500/ $600–750**

- Always check every small pot in boxes of "junk" bottles on the floor at fairs and car boot sales.
- Damage is acceptable due to rarity of all but the commonest half-dozen types.
- Beware of imitations – check out current bottle literature (see *p* 60).

▼ Clarke's Miraculous Salve

This small pot is one of the six most easily discovered types, but this rare example has the original top covering and contents. Such a discovery makes it highly desirable. It claims to cure "... boils, abscesses/fistulas, bad breasts and gatherings of all kinds". It was available in three sizes priced at 1/1d, 2/9d, and 4/6d. The larger two sizes are very rare.

Full and labelled Clarke's Miraculous Salve, 1/1d size, c.1910–20, **£60–80/$90–120**, (without contents **£12–15/ $18–20**; larger sizes, **£60–120/$90–180**)

Dr Rooke's Golden Ointment, 4.5cm (1¾in) tall, c.1880–1900, **£300–500/$450–750**

▲ Dr Rooke's Golden Ointment

Scarborough was a prosperous Yorkshire seaside resort in the Victorian times. "Dr Rooke's Golden Ointment" no doubt capitalized upon the curative appeal of seaside bathing and came only in the 2/9d size, a large amount in those days. Though this is a c.1880–1900 example, the transfer claims the formula was discovered 30 or 40 years earlier, presumably to give more credibility.

▼ Mrs Croft's Ointment

West Handley, a small township in Derbyshire, north England, seems an unlikely source for a transferred ointment pot. This ointment was quite possibly a local concoction gaining an element of success in the area, but judging by the pot's rarity today it failed to spread nationwide. Regional rarities are part of the appeal of seeking out and digging remote dumps, ever optimistic of finding such scarce localized collectables.

Mrs Croft's Ointment, both c.1880–1900. Left: 7½p size, **£60–80/$90–120**; right: 1 sh. size, **£120–150/$180–225**

Poison bottles

For centuries the containment of poisons, acids, and other such dangerous chemicals has been a subject not to be taken lightly. Accidental consumption of toxic substances forced Parliament to legislate. After November 1st 1863 it became illegal in Britain to sell any poisonous substance not "... supplied in a glass phial or bottle of hexagonal shape, of which five sides shall be fluted, and on the remaining side thereof a label shall be affixed with the word 'poison' and directions for use distinctly marked thereon." Within twenty years, inventors were creating a wealth of weird and wonderful patent and novelty ideas, providing today's collectors with one of the most fascinating and colourful areas in the bottle collecting field.

Left to right: Wilson's patent, 27ml (1fl oz), c.1900, **£120–150/ $180–225**; standard 115ml (4fl oz) hexagonal, with Fletcher's "poison guard" patent, c.1900–20, **£20–30/$30–45**, (without guard, **£2/$3**); sheared lip, cobalt 55ml (2fl oz), c.1900–10, **£15–20/$20–30**

▶ **Poison trio**
Wilson's patent of March 17th 1899 was for a glass container with "one or more of the sides being grooved or corrugated". The Nottingham area, central England, is a good source for these bottles. Green hexagonals are common and a standard design used right up to the late 1940s at first made in blue, then green, and finally amber. The cobalt sheared lip hexagonal is unique to Scotland.

▼ **Skull poison**
Carlton H. Lee, Boston, Massachusetts patented the skull poison, one of the most spectacular of all late Victorian bottles, in 1894. The US Patent Office design number 23,399 records "the body of which has in general the configuration of a human skull ... at the bottom of the body appears the representation of cross bones." There are three known sizes and the smallest, 7cm (2¾in), is regarded as the rarest.

Skull poison, small size, c.1900, **£1,200–1,500/ $1,800–2,250**, (complete set of three, **£5,000– 7,000/$7,500 –10,500**)

Did you know?
There is a widely held misconception that poison bottles were ribbed to warn off blind people. This is untrue. Bottles with dangerous contents bore ribs for identification in the dark as most households were lit by gas, oil lamps, or candles.

Submarine poisons, cobalt, c.1910. Left: 11.5cm (4¾in) long, **£500–700/$750–1,050**; centre: 10cm (4in) long, **£300–400/$450–600**; right: 7.5cm (3in) long, **£300–400/$450–600**

▲ Submarine poisons

This bottle gets its name from its boatlike appearance. It was registered in 1899 by G. W. Walker and H. J. Martin, though it was not granted Letters Patent until 1906. The specification describes these bottles as "... made with their necks situated between the ends, instead of at one end of the bottle." A number were found in Yorkshire in the 1970s, although a few have surfaced in other areas of Britain. Beware of examples repaired at the ends, due to very thin glass.

▼ Martin's patent

A. W. Martin patented a unique bottle shape in 1902 "... for enclosing poisons and other dangerous liquids, disinfectants and the like ... will only lay upon one side, and the contents will not escape ... should the cork be removed". Most have been found in the Manchester area, northwest England, in nine sizes ranging from the rare 14ml (½fl oz) up to the unique 560ml (20fl oz) capacity. Only one is currently known in green; all the rest are standard aqua or an ice blue tinged glass.

A 27ml (1fl oz) capacity Martin's poison patent, aqua glass, c.1902–10, **£150–200/$225–300**

Langford's coffin poison bottle, 1871, **£4,000–5,000/$6,000–8,500**

▲ Coffin poison

This stunning bottle is the most desirable British poison patent. To date only four have been recorded. In 1871, G. F. Langford was given provisional patent protection for a bottle "... in the shape of a coffin, and maybe externally ornamented with a death's head or other device". Similar-shaped bottles were patented in America in 1876 and 1890. Striking poison bottle designs must at times have proved a novelty attraction to an unsuspecting toddler, luring them to an early grave, making them somehow self-defeating.

Pot lids

Rapidly expanding towns and cities worldwide in the 1860s and 1870s created an enormous need for prepackaged food and a wide variety of other products. Potted meat, bear's grease (see *p.44*), toothpaste, cold cream, salves, and the like came in underglaze-printed pot lids and bases, mass-produced in the bustling Staffordshire potteries. The fascinating and lively designs, and ornate graphic layout, represent one of the largest groups of collectables. There are thousands of different examples, and most people either specialize in one product or seek out pieces from their own region. Bear's grease has proved the most consistently collected group of pot lids, and this is reflected in their ever-spiralling cost.

▼ Multicoloured pot lids
Multicoloured pot lids are often referred to as "Pratt lids", after one of the main manufacturers *(see Fact File)*. With the mid-Victorian technique for producing high-quality, full colour images they became a veritable canvas for all manner of national and international events.

Windsor Park (returning from stag hunting), 10cm (4in) diam., c.1850, **£150–200/ $225–300**

▲ Fish paste
Prior to a national railway system, fresh fish was not available in most inland towns. A vinegar mix increased the shelf life and proved a popular sandwich spread. This example has a "damper" to compress the remaining contents and keep it moist, but effectively providing less spread in the pot.

Yarmouth Bloater Paste, with damper and base, 9cm (3¾in), c.1880–1900, **£100–120/ $150–180**, (no damper, **£50–70/ $75–105**)

Trouchet's Corn Cure, 5cm (2in)
diam., c.1870–1900,
£30–40/$45–60

▼ Philadelphia shaving cream

A select number of American towns appear to have taken on board the concept of pot lids as a packaging technique, primarily for shaving creams. Philadelphia became a very important centre for shaving cream production. This example in red print is typical of their high-quality designs. Some of the finest pictorial pot lids from the 1870s and 1880s were made by American companies, and are equally prized in Britain and America.

Bazin's "Unrivalled Premium Shaving Cream", 8cm (3½in) diam., c.1880–1900, **£120–150/ $180–225**

▲ Trouchet's Corn Cure

Bare feet rubbing against ill-fitting shoes led to constant problems for the poor in the 19thC, especially manual workers. The abundance of so many corn cure pot lids in Australia suggests that the intense heat exacerbated this ailment. Judging by the large number of Trouchet pot lids found in Australia, it appears to have been a long-selling market leader there for a considerable period.

FACT FILE

Multicoloured pot lids
Jesse Austin and Felix Pratt perfected a complex multicoloured transferred process in the 1870s, the middle of Queen Victoria's reign, creating full-colour popular images of the day. The technique was fiddly, coining the term "pratting about" meaning fussy or over complex.

▼ Boots Cold Cream

Town life and a rich social calendar increased the demand for a wide range of beauty products, and Cold Cream for the skin became extremely popular from the 1880s onwards. Jesse Boot's entrepreneurial skills generated outlets in Nottingham, Sheffield, and Lincoln, and his expansion and success has continued unabated to the present day.

Boots Cold Cream, 7cm (2¾in) diam., c.1880–1920, **£15–20/$20–30**

▼ Gosnell's Tooth Paste

Young Queen Victoria's profile was used most effectively by John Gosnell and Co., London, to promote their Cherry Tooth Paste. Judging by the number of lids dug in Britain, South Africa, and Australasia, it appears to have been a bestselling toothpaste brand. Whether the range of subtle coloured lid transfers led to such success is a matter of conjecture. However, by 1900–10 they gave in to market pressure and adopted black and white designs, as used by their competitors.

Gosnell's Cherry Tooth Paste, 7.7cm (3¼in), c.1890–1900, **£20–30/$30–45**

▼ Cheesman's Rat Poison

In the late 1950s/early 1960s, the upwardly mobile middle classes moved away from the overcrowded cities for a cleaner country life. Flagged kitchens were replaced by concrete and the new linoleum covering, a trend which today has gone full circle – back to the original flags. Fashion and style aside, kitchens in late Victorian and early Edwardian times harboured vermin, necessitating the need for rat poison. This was quite a late product judging by the house design and telephone number.

Cheesman's Rat Poison, Brighton, 9cm (3¼in), c.1910–1920, **£200–300/$300–450**

Véritable Graisse D'Ours, blue pot lid and base, 6.5cm (2¾in), c.1760–70, **£170–200/$255–300**

▲ Véritable Graisse D'Ours

Bear's grease was popular in England from the 17thC, claiming efficacy in promoting healthy hair growth, though its high cost restricted its use to more affluent societies. Many thousands of brown Russian bears were killed for its production. James Atkinson, 24 Old Bond Street, London, was the most successful manufacturer, from 1799 up to 1934. Other companies competed, including the French firm who made this lid and highly decorated base, which is noticeably different from the norm.

Collecting tips
● Beware of modern
transferred reproductions.
● Damage tends to
affect all the edge areas
– inspect this carefully.
● Varnished fakes with
a paper image stuck
onto a damaged old lid
can be easily detected
using the finger nail at
the perimeter.

▼ M. F. Thompson tooth paste

The vast majority of
pot lids were circular.
However, square and
rectangular examples are the
second most frequently-found
shapes. The number of
Scottish pot lids recorded,
despite most being quite rare,
increases as digging "north of
the border" continues to
produce new finds. This very
rare square example features
the Scott monument on
Edinburgh's Princes Street,
and was recovered by a diver
from an undisclosed loch.
An even more rare variation
of this pictorial pot lid is
found on a rectangular shape.

M. F. Thompson, Edinburgh, 6.5 x
5.5cm (2¾ x 2¼in) c.1880–1900,
£300–400/$450–600

Tooth paste, 7.5cm (3in), c.1880–
1900, **£150–200/$225–300**

▲ Coloured cherries pot lid

After 1880, most companies
resorted to the lower-cost
process of black transfer on a
white base. However, in order
to stand out from the crowd,
some firms adopted different
coloured transfers and/or a
coloured background. A few
designs incorporated hand-
applied coloured sections as
well, usually over the final
glaze, such as on these leaves
and cherries. Unfortunately,
due to years of being
buried in tips this area
is more prone to wear,
making it crucial to seek
out top quality examples.

Toilet Powder, with original
puff, 10cm (4in) tall,
c.1920–30, **£200–250/
$300–375**, (without
contents, **£150–200/
$225–300**)

▼ John Gosnell's Cherry Blossom Toilet Powder

After almost five decades of
worldwide dump digging and
various specialist-related
publications, the bottle hobby
is now far more aware of what
has been found and recorded,
along with the relative rarity
of each item. Collectors are
therefore excited by finds
which veer from the norm,
as in the case of this unusually
pretty, elaborately transferred
pink background pot lid and
base. This design was replaced
by an identical design
manufactured in a printed tin.

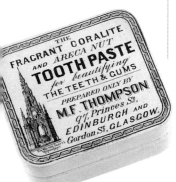

Quack cures

An unromantic image of Victorian life is conjured up as an easily duped public gurgling down proprietary medicines, which claimed to cure nearly everything. Child mortality was high and hygiene standards low. Medics of the day lapsed into generalities for diagnosis and treatment. Illiteracy was high, and not surprisingly the sick turned to ready-made medicines, accepting the label, or circular claims, with a sometimes blind faith. Quacks peddled bottled medicines from town to town, luring crowds with circus-like sideshows, culminating with the hard sell. The range of "quack cure" bottles is broad and varied.

Daffy's Elixir, pontilled, olive green glass, 11cm (4½in), c.1820–40, **£600–800/$1000–1,200**, (aqua, non-pontilled, c.1870–90, **£60–80/$90–120**)

▶ **Daffy's Elixir**
Around the time of the Great Plague of London in 1665 and the Great Fire of 1666 Daffy's Elixir appeared: one of the most successful and widely copied patent "cure-alls" sold in Britain and America. Its success carried it through to the end of Queen Victoria's reign in 1901. Early coloured, pontilled examples, such as this near-perfect bottle, are rare and highly sought after. Later non-pontilled aqua glass versions are slightly easier to find.

▼ **Warner's Safe Cure**
H. H. Warner inherited a safe-making factory, but chose to pursue a business in quackery. All bottles featured a pictorial safe, and within ten years his American production had spread to London, Toronto, Melbourne, and Frankfurt.

All c.1880–1900. Left to right: two-pint, amber London Warner's Safe Cure, 26cm (10¾in), **£500–600/$750–1000**; miniature green Warner's, 11cm (4½in), **£300–400/$450–600**; one-pint, dark green Diabetes Cure, 12cm (5in), **£170–200/$255–300**

William Radam's Microbe Killer, amber glass, 26cm (10¾in), c.1890–1905, **£120–150/$180–225**

▲ Radam's Microbe Killer

Another infamous medicine was Radam's Microbe Killer, claiming the cure for cancer, consumption, yellow fever, diphtheria, and jaundice. The impressive large square amber bottle displays a man clubbing a skeleton, driving out the microbes. "Kills all Diseases" is printed on the base.

When analyzed in 1906 it was found to contain nothing more than 99 percent water, plus small quantities of sulphuric acid, hydrochloric acid, and a wine-based colouring agent.

▼ Fisher's Seaweed Extract

Most late Victorian quack cures enjoyed regional patriotism, no doubt playing on the adage "better the devil you know". There were many doubts about the efficacy (or not) of brand leaders. One such parochial medicine was Fisher's Seaweed Extract, from the Lake District, a sheep-farming area in northwest England, purporting to cure farmer's aches and pains. The striking shape no doubt attracted attention and aided sales. However, discovery throughout Britain has been sparse, suggesting minimal or short-lived success.

Fisher's Seaweed Extract, green glass, 13cm (5¼in), c.1880–1900, **£150–200/$225–300**

Price's Glycerin, full and labelled one-pint, cobalt wedge-shaped bottle, 19cm (7¾in), c.1880–1900, **£200–250/ $300–375**

▶ Price's Glycerin

Successful quack charlatans were evidently aware of the importance of the visual impact of their packaged products. "Price's Glycerin" adopted a vibrant cobalt blue bottle, which, judging by its widespread discovery, sold well. Patented in 1885, it won medals at Paris Exhibitions, and the Grand Prix in 1889 and 1900. The one-pint bottle (empty) is a classic collectable, but the two-pint size is especially elusive. Look out for examples with their original blue stopper.

Pharmacy

The Pharmaceutical Society of Great Britain was formed in 1841, and by the following year a register of approved chemists and druggists was set up to steer society away from the charlatans with no medical training. Many pharmacists packed their own remedies and sold them alongside nationally advertised patent and proprietary medicines. Pharmacies dispensed a wide range of goods, offered counter lines such as toiletries and invalid and infant foods, and also sauces, pickles, tea, spices, dyes, ink, candles, matches, tobacco, and aerated waters – a vast array of household items not associated with modern pharmacies. This category is almost limitless. Many collectors tend to specialize in one field such as eye baths or baby feeders, or across the board with a particular date.

Grip Tight feeder bottle, original box and teats, box 12cm (5in) long, c.1940–50, **£15–20/ $20–30**

▲ Baby feeders

Early teats were made from pickled calves' udders and wired onto pottery boat-shaped feeding bottles. Hygiene was poor, and the history of baby feeder designs is littered with catastrophes. This double-ended banana-shaped feeder was a finale to all previous improvements. Interestingly, some Victorian ideas have recently been rekindled.

▼ Eye baths or eye cups

Poor sanitation and hygiene in the 19thC led to regular eye infections. Eye bath and lotions cleaned and soothed. Early blue-and-white pottery or silver ones are now rare, reflected in high prices. Most of the large glass selection, however, can form the basis of a relatively inexpensive collection (amber ones are the rarest), taking up little space. Early hand-blown and unusual coloured types are rising rapidly in value.

Left to right: blue-and-white ceramic, c.1820–40, **£800–1,200/ $1,200– 1,800**; amber embossed, c.1920–40, **£30–50/ $45–75**; cobalt reservoir type, c.1890–1900, **£80–120/ $120–180**

▼ Inhalers

Inhalers facilitated the entry of a remedy, in the form of a vapour or fine spray, to either the nose or mouth (or both). Dr John Mudge patented a pewter inhaler in 1778 but it was the pottery types which gained widespread popularity, epitomized by this late Victorian decorative Boval example. Less elaborate types, such as those by S. Maw Son & Thompson and Dr Nelson, can still be purchased for less than £20/$30 each. Try to find examples with the cork and both glass tubes.

Brown and black transferred Boval Inhaler, 16cm (6¼in) to lid top, c.1880–90, **£150–200/$225–300**

Left to right: pontilled shop round, paper label, 12cm (5in), c.1880–1920, **£15–20/ $20–30**; label under glass with metal cover, 25cm (10in), c.1910–20, **£40–60/$60–90**

▲ Shop rounds

From the 17thC up to the 1950s, shop rounds (used for storing various ingredients) came in a large variety of sizes, with different stoppers, and names on paper stuck onto the bottle or on clear, brown, blue, or green labels under glass (blue lined ones are rare). Some glasshouses continued hand-making long after others had automated manufacture, making dating quite difficult. Bright blue or green, pontilled labels under glass types are the most desirable.

▼ Counter tray

Imagine an original Victorian pharmacy with a polished mahogany counter, Latin-inscribed wooden drawers lining the walls, and shiny brass scales in one corner and a paraffin stove in another. In such a place you would find a grandiose ceramic counter top, such as this American one, upon which to place your order or pick up your change.

"Sparks' Perfect Health" counter top tray, 25cm (10in), c.1860–80, **£700–800/$1,000–1,200**

Early stoneware

High-fired stoneware pottery is an extremely resilient, durable material. It was ideally suited to all manner of utilitarian containers fuelled by the avaricious and buoyant British economy in the mid to late 19thC. Perfected much earlier in the Far East, stoneware pottery was widely used in Britain by the early 1800s, with a natural London production base on the Thames embankment. At the height of Victoria's reign, *c.*1870s, filthy black smoke emanated from many bottle ovens in central Britain, around Derbyshire and Staffordshire. Drinks-related containers abound in this category. Simple, mostly undecorated, handmade stoneware objects up to 150 years old can still be purchased for less than £10/$15.

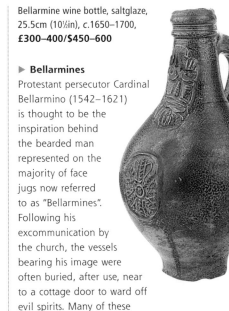

Bellarmine wine bottle, saltglaze, 25.5cm (10¼in), c.1650–1700, **£300–400/$450–600**

▶ **Bellarmines**
Protestant persecutor Cardinal Bellarmino (1542–1621) is thought to be the inspiration behind the bearded man represented on the majority of face jugs now referred to as "Bellarmines". Following his excommunication by the church, the vessels bearing his image were often buried, after use, near to a cottage door to ward off evil spirits. Many of these early wine jugs were made in Germany and Flanders from the mid 1500s, and later in England, up to the late 1700s.

▼ **Reform flasks**
In England the 1832 Reform Act was the true beginning of democracy, heralding better conditions for working classes. Political leaders, royalty, and more were immortalized in semi-figural spirit flasks. These were made at London and Derbyshire potteries. Over 100 variations are known. Rare pieces include this flask, promoting a specific wine merchant.

Lord Brougham reform, Sheffield named, 18cm (7in), c.1830–40, **£300–400/ $450–600**, (without merchant name, **£170–200/ $255–300**)

• Saltglaze is a red–brown orange peel effect achieved by throwing rock salt into the kiln at the height of the firing process; effectively, but unevenly coating the surface.

• Grey–green slip items are made by dipping unfired objects into a vessel of liquid "slip", thereby coating the clay form.

Dabell slab sealed porter, Nottingham, c.1840–50, **£300–400/$450–600**

▲ Dabell slab seal

Nottingham, then Sheffield, boasts the largest number of different mid-Victorian flasks bearing applied pie crust-like adornments called "slab seals", impressed with the proprietor's name. The greater number of lines, the more desirable the piece. These mostly Northern ale or porter flasks were made by the Oldfield pottery at Chesterfield. The Railway Bell hostelry in Nottingham used several designs, all now rare. Simple, early grey-green glazed, impressed porters, c.1830–50, can be purchased for a fraction of their slab sealed counterparts.

▼ Veterinary flask

Illustrating the ability of pottery manufacturers to both diversify their styles and broaden their market is this flat-bodied flask featuring a ribbed neck. The top seal is impressed "I. Gaskell Veterinary Surgeon Bolton", and the lower slab is an extremely rare cut out shape depicting a horse. Veterinary flasks are much more scarce than ale examples; only a handful have been recorded, including a few cow pictorials, and are consequently highly prized.

Unique pictorial Bolton veterinary flask, 14cm (5½in), c.1830–50, **£500–700/$750–1,000**

Dark brown, saltglaze spirit barrel, 25cm (10in), c.1840–60, **£80–120/$120–180**

▲ Spirit barrels

A variety of barrel shapes can be found, most with bulging sides. Different decorations were applied including sprigs, creeping vines and coats of arms, and on a central band was painted the contents of the barrel. This unusual straight-sided item has original paint traces.

Water filters

Household luxuries such as turning on a tap have been around for less than 100 years. Even today, such basics are still lacking in some countries. In Britain the cholera epidemic of 1866 revealed a stark need for better sanitation, and general hygiene improvements and clean water became a priority. Water filters used various means to decrease contamination of well and stream water, though sometimes the simplest perforated ceramic layers held back little more than the largest grubs and beetles! Carbon blocks, cloth, charcoal, sand, and even concrete were utilized, but maybe the safest ally was a higher natural level of immunity. Although quite large and heavy, water filters are visually interesting even without their lids, and can be used as stylish household plant containers!

Waisted Lipscombe & Co. filter, 32cm (13in) tall, c.1850–60, **£120–150/ $180–225**

▼ Lipscombe & Co.

This waisted filter design was a popular model from c.1840–60. Ornamental sprigging decorates the entire body and lid, while impressed lettering is picked out in black: "Lipscombe & Co. / Patentees / 44 Queen Victoria St / Mansion House / London / and at Temple Bar." On the underside of the lid the throwing rings (see p.59) indicate it was handmade, possibly on a potter's wheel and manually turned by a young boy, or maybe a foot-operated kick wheel. This item was recovered from a bramble bush, using a plank of wood.

▶ Cheavin's filter

This filter has an elaborate transfer at the front with the wording "Pasteur System / The / Cheavin Microbe Proof / Filter / Manufactured by / The Fulham Pottery / and / Cheavin Filter Coy / Fulham / London / SW." Many potteries were located on or around the Thames embankment, though by 1900, when smoke was less tolerated, many were urged to relocate. Unique pictorially transferred filters, c.1900–20, were exported to Australasia.

Cheavin Microbe Proof filter, 38cm (15in) tall, c.1870–1910, **£120–150/ $180–225**

- Most water filters are missing their original lid. Without these, values should be halved.
- Sometimes the lids fit poorly because the inner filter lining is missing, though this does not generally affect the price.
- Minor damage and no spigot (see p.59) are generally acceptable.

▼ Battersea filter

Large volumes of hand-thrown filters were manufactured from c.1830 up to the turn of the 20thC, London being the main production centre. Male potters hand-threw, on a piece-rate system, while women did the decorating. Although filters vary considerably in size, most featured two integral side carrying handles. This "Silicated Carbon Filter / Works Battersea / London" is a rare south-of-the-river item – strikingly similar to Doulton artware types (see right).

Silicated carbon filter, Battersea, 35cm (14in) tall, c.1880–1900, **£200–250/$300–375**

Doulton artware filter, 32cm (13in) tall, c.1880–1900, **£400–600/$600–900**

▲ Doulton filter

Having provided the saltglazed drainpipes for London's sewer system, Henry Doulton built a water and sanitation related manufacturing business, creating some of the finest artware water filters. At the age of 17, as a trainee, Doulton "threw fifteen 3 gallon water filters before breakfast", while as late as 1953 Doulton were exporting filters to Fiji. The typically shaped Doulton artware filter shown here features a "bung", which tastefully disguises the tap area when not in use.

▼ Permutit softener

The "Permutit / Water Softener", available in three sizes, had a Royal Warrant, and proved very popular in London and other "hard water" areas. Worth mentioning are tradesmen's miniature sample filters, used to promote sales in hardware stores. They are among the most prized filters.

Permutit water softener, 32cm (13in) tall, c.1920–40, **£20–30/$30–45**

Water jugs

Although water jugs, as such, date back to early times, this category generally refers to jugs produced specifically for the promotion of beer or whisky. From the 1840s, the beer jug served up frothy ale drawn first from the barrel, then poured from a jug into a pewter tankard, black jack (see *p.*59), or other suitable container. By the 1870s, the commercial sale of whisky became widespread, necessitating small jugs to dispense water, which brought out the flavour of the whisky. Pottery, glass, and metal jugs were made in a variety of sizes, styles, and shapes, providing a rich legacy for today's collectors. This specialist field has witnessed phenomenal growth in people chasing the elusive rarities, resulting in fantastic rises in value.

Barnsley Brewery, Doulton Burslem jug, 17cm (6¾in), c.1906, **£1,200–1,500/ $1,800–2,250**

▶ **Barnsley Brewery**

Nothing is new! Even 100 years ago, it was not unusual for a jug to promote its contents as well as other products. Just as a cereal packet today may advertise train tickets, this Doulton Burslem-made jug for Oakwell Brewery used both side panels to promote Brown Corbett Distillers from Ireland and Scotland's Edward Young & Co. whisky. It is regarded as one of the world's finest advertising jugs ever made.

▼ **Dewar's**

John Dewar set up as a wine merchant in Scotland in 1846, becoming the first man to commercially bottle his own whisky brand. Royal warranty in 1893 gave it universal approval, and greater success. Doulton subtly modified traditional hunting ware saltglaze stoneware jugs into bar-top promotions for Dewar's, by adding a dark green top, plus transferred and applied lettering. Sizes ranged from 5cm (2in) to 15cm (6in), manufactured from 1880 to 1930.

Green topped Dewar's water jug, 11cm (4½in), c.1893–1901, **£150–200/ $225–300**

Craigellachie Distillery, "Gaelic Old Smuggler Whisky", Doulton Burslem, 18cm (7in), c.1910–20, **£600–700/$900–1,000**

▲ Glenlivet

The style of this jug, with its mustard body, was unique to Doulton's Burslem factory, but unfortunately the earthenware body is more prone to damage and staining than the sturdier stoneware jugs. Several variations are recorded, this one featuring a detailed, romanticized transfer of the distillery beneath the lip, and wording to both sides. A number of other companies adopted this distinctive Doulton style, in a range of shapes. All are now considered rare, though some are not pictorial.

▼ Johnnie Walker

Once a humble Kilmarnock grocer, John Walker started a sideline which eventually consumed his entire business. Supplying whisky to Glaswegian sailors, the brand name blossomed, receiving five Australian accolades between 1880 and 1897, and it is still going strong today. One of the largest, most impractical, but impressive bar jugs was this 1920s Ashtead Pottery creation. Water jugs by their very nature need only be small, but larger ones evolved, presumably to outdo their rivals.

Ashtead Pottery Johnnie Walker bar jug, c.1920s, 39cm (15½in), **£500–700/$750–1,000**

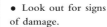

* Look out for signs of damage.
* Modern, made-up designs on jugs never used for promotion by whisky or beer manufacturers are frowned upon.
* "Wade Regicor London England" is a Wade base mark used from 1950–60 and provides a wide range of affordable jugs, if the early types are too expensive.

"Drink McNish's Special Whisky", 18.5cm (7½in), c.1880–90, **£500–600/$750–900**

▲ McNish's

One of the most attractive late Victorian whisky jugs is this Dunn Bennett, Burslem-made rarity. Today we may be confused about what we should and should not consume; this product claimed to be "the medical whisky of the world". This was, of course, long before Trading Standards.

Whisky crocks

The Victorian years witnessed huge changes in lifestyle and outlook. Increased travel opportunities saw people in Britain leaving their families to seek fame and fortune in far-flung places. The Gold Rush drew men to hot regions where a diet of salted meat and boiled potatoes was washed down with whisky. Pre-1860 whisky crock exports were in traditional saltglaze, but by the 1880s the brighter Bristol glaze was predominant and these were covered in ornate, often pictorial or coloured transfers, and have become today's prized pieces. The firms of Doulton, Port Dundas, H. Kennedy, Buchans, and Stiff all made crocks. Some examples can still be found for under £50/$75, though rarer items cost a lot more.

Sunderland Grant Mackay, Doulton Lambeth, 17.5cm (6⅞in), c.1898, **£500–1,500/ $750–2,250**

▼ Sunderland Grant Mackay

Typically, the Doulton Lambeth artists created the finest of all stoneware whisky jugs, emblazoned with applied bands and friezes, and the vibrant "Doulton blue" glaze. This flask is the smallest of three sizes, with a slightly less desirable grey-blue body glaze. The best hunting ground for such "gems" is North America and Australia, because they were specially made for export to these countries. Unfortunately these types rarely appear on the open market – hence the broad price guide.

▶ Forty Second

Certain crocks seem inexplicably difficult and elusive to track down, suggesting either a small limited number made, or a particularly short-lived brand name. This crock is one such example. My own research lists some surfacing on the eastern side of Canada, a few in New Zealand, and just two in Scotland. This particular "skirted" shape is one of the rarest and most desirable forms, appearing on only a small number of different named crocks. The term "NB" in the transfer denotes "North Britain".

Forty Second Fine Highland Whisky, 18.5cm (7½in), c.1890–1900, **£500–600/ $750–900**

- These items are called crocks, jugs, flasks, flagons, or jars.
- Scottish whisky is usually spelt without an "e", Irish "whiskey" often with.
- It is believed that enjoying partaking of a "wee dram" helps in the appreciation of this specialist collecting field!

▼ Galway Bay

The "Galway Bay" is one of the few transferred crocks made in the "mallet" shape. Most collectors believe all stoneware crocks were made in Britain and filled before worldwide export. However, it has been proved conclusively that certain examples were made in America. This crock, transferred "Galway Bay / Export / Irish Whisky", is one such example and quite possibly mould-made as opposed to hand thrown.

Mallet-shaped "Galway Bay" crock, 17.5cm (6⅞in), c.1910–20, **£150–200/$225–300**

Blue transferred "Auld Lang Syne", 18.2cm (7¼in), c.1890–1900, **£400–600/$600–900**, (black print, **£50–60/$75–90**)

▲ Auld Lang Syne

Robbie Burns' famous poem (and song) is immortalized on this highly detailed transferred tavern scene of three men playing cards and drinking in front of a fire. The black transferred example is not rare, but this blue crock is one of only six yet to be found. A later variant with straight sides can still be found for under £50/$75, while the pottery company Weideman in Cleveland, Ohio, also packaged the brand in American-made jugs.

▼ Rabbie Burns

How better to make a wanderlust Scottish gold miner homesick than sell him a jug depicting a farmer standing by his ploughing horse and faithful dog? Enough to drive any man to drink. A rare crock made by H. Kennedy, Glasgow, now discovered predominantly in Australia.

Two-tone "Rabbie Burns Whisky" jar, 19cm (7⅜in), c.1900–20, **£400–500/$600–750**

Fakes and forgeries

Popularity of any collecting field attracts fraudsters, quick to pounce upon a keen and eager fraternity. The bottle world has attracted unscrupulous attentions, though sometimes unintentional. Up-to-date information in specialist magazines enables the shrewd collector to stay one step ahead of potential pitfalls. All too often forgeries disappear from the scene as quickly as they appeared, replaced by fresh scams. Be forewarned.

The National Bottle Museum, Elsecar, houses one of the largest gatherings of fakes and forgeries. Never be duped by the presence of fakes at antique fairs, which often command high prices.

black glass sealed wines Be aware of old seals (from broken bottles) reglued to plain unsealed shapes.

clay pipes Still made, they tend to wipe clean easily, have no natural age, wear, or patina, and feature pronounced mould seams.

codds Still made in the Far East in a variety of forms, some even with plastic lips. The heavier examples emanate from India, still sold by street vendors, and come with blue marbles in the neck or coloured body swirls. There are even black glass examples. Bases on these tend to be thick and uneven.

coloured lacquer By far the most commonly encountered alteration to low cost aqua items is to make bottles appear like higher-valued rarities by applying an outer lacquer coloured coating, which makes the surface less cold and when held up to natural light reveals inconsistent colour density. A gentle scrape, underneath, with a metal object (coin) should scratch the fake surface. Inks, syphons, and codds are the most popular choices.

cream pots The same instigator of the coloured top Rishton g.b.'s ordered a quantity of "Imperial Creamery Glasgow" pots. Transfer quality is very poor indeed.

enamel signs Copies of famous images are popular kitchen adornments. Picture quality is usually poor (but getting better), and the backs display tell-tale cog marks from modern production methods.

eye baths Modern coloured examples in glass (some with swirls) and plastic are easily avoided with a little knowledge.

ginger beers A few have been made in recent years. Pearson's of Chesterfield produced some in the 1960s for Habitat. These are easily discernible from older types, with a very dark brown top (not tan), and a base transfer (sometimes scratched off). Blue and green top "Barraclough/Rishton" g.b.'s were made by Buchan in the 1980s and have a lion trademark of poor picture quality. Reglazed tops on old g.b.'s attempt to create scarce blue or green tops, normally with a tell-tale runny glaze.

hamiltons Pink, and other colours, have come from the Far East, with incorrect blob lips. Schweppes embossed aqua hamiltons tend to feature plenty of air bubbles, and are slightly longer than originals.

night lights Coloured figurals are recorded, but are not easily detected. Non-figurals, made for modern-day use, tend to be much heavier and minus the rough/sheared lip.

pot lids Watch out for the following: paper labels lacquered over on old plain lids (a fingernail under the edge detects the paper); brand new ones are not easy to spot for the uninitiated, but bottle shows dissuade sales of these items, and stallholders will offer sound advice.

pub jugs Modern examples, often old adverts simply transferred to new jugs. These are generally not collected by those interested in old items specifically made for promotion by the brewery and whisky companies.

reform flasks Bourne Denby made a set of flasks for export in the 1960s. Colour and weight are wrong, as is the back stamp.

saltglaze House shapes, flasks, and pistols, tend to have thin, slip-cast lips. The lip should be thick and chunky, the inside almost vertical, and not echoing the outside curved shape. Copies tend to be less heavy than originals.

Warner's Safe Cure Three different copies are known:
• Green pint, with label. Base embossed with gift company who commissioned them.
• Frank's Kidney & Liver Cure is simply a fatter-looking bottle, intended to deceive nobody.
• A range of oddly coloured Warners from the Far East all featuring the wrong top; the inside echoes the outside curve shape, instead of the heavy chunky blob lip.

Glossary

A.b.m. Automatic Bottle Machine Developed by Michael Owens in 1903, and gradually led to the demise of hand made glass bottles.

Anneal An essential glass manufacturing process gradually cooling items to room temperature in an oven or lehr.

aqua cheaply made Victorian or Edwardian glass tinged with light green/light blue appearance, presumably named after its resemblance to water

Bottologist Collective name given to a collector of bottles.

black glass very dark glass, usually green or brown when held up to the light

black jack large leathern cup, or can, for drink

blob lip/blob top heavy knob-like lip finish to pottery or glass, developed for regular reuse

c.c. (crown cap) invented in 1892. A metal closure, with cork liner, which clasped round the thin glass or pottery rim, opened with a bottle opener

ch. abbreviation for champagne. A shape describing a particular style, generally pottery ginger beer

bottles, tall with a gradually narrowing shoulder up to the lip

free-blown glass made by hand and tool manipulation, without the aid of moulds

g.b. abbreviation for ginger beer bottle

mallet free-blown wine bottle shape, c.1725–60, shaped like a woodworker's mallet

onion free-blown glass bottle shape, c.1690–1720, like an onion in shape

pontil glass rod pressed into the bottom of a handmade bottle to support it while the lip area was finished. When snapped off, the pontil left a rough and uneven finish, sometimes jagged and sharp

quack charlatan or imposter who recommended secret remedies knowing them to be worthless

saltglaze cheapest form of glazing in a single firing process – throwing rock salt into the kiln when white hot, igniting, and applying an attractive, orange peel-like, red/red-brown/brown finish

sheared lip jagged lip finish created in manufacture to enable corks to be pressed into the top to seal, before being dipped into a

wax covering

Sick glass Bottles recovered from a dump where ground acids have altered the surface to an unpleasant, white, milky finish.

spigot wooden or metal tap inserted into flagons, barrels, filters, etc

st (standard) most common ginger beer bottle shape with straight sides and a pronounced, short, angular shoulder

stoneware pottery fired to between 1,250 and 1,280 degrees centigrade, does not absorb water or any liquid

S.s. Swing stopper In 1875 Charles De Quillfeldt patented a metal lever device, with a pottery lid which swung open and closed easily. Used by corona into the 1960's, and still found on some trendy European lagers and beers.

throwing rings lines inside a pottery object left by the hand of the potter who "threw" the item on a potter's wheel

tt (two-tone) pottery term where the top section is tan coloured, and the lower part a light creamy tone

What to read

Unfortunately, the highly specialist nature of this category means there is one principal publisher, and a number of self-published titles, though this list is extended to provide a good general basis for reading. Some titles may be available at libraries and at good, large bookshops; otherwise check out www.onlinebbr.com for an up-to-date book listing.

Derek Askey
Stoneware Bottles
(BBR Publishing, 1999)

Dennis Ashurst
The History of South Yorkshire Glass
(Sheffield University, 1975)
Chris Baylee & Andrew Morley
Street Jewellery
(New Cavendish, 1988)
Alan Blakeman
Advertising Pot Lids
(BBR Publishing, 1998)
*Antique Bottle Collectors'
Encyclopedia* (BBR Publishing, 1997)
Ginger Beers (BBR Publishing, 1998)
Reform Flasks
(BBR Publishing, 1997)
R. Dennis *1898 trade catalogue
facsimile* (Farrow & Jackson, 1997)

Dunn, R. & J.
Codd, the Man, the Bottle
(R. Dunn, 2000)
Gaimster, D. *German Stoneware
1200–1900* (BBR Publishing, 1998)
Keith Gretton
Advertising Collectables
(BBR Publishing, 1989)
Russ Harrison
Mineral Water Closures
(Harrison Publishing, 1989)
Robin Hildyard
Browne Muggs (Victoria & Albert
Museum, London, 1985)
Michael Jones
Time Gentlemen Please

(Public Record Office, 1998)
Jocelyn Lukins
Collecting Doultonware
(Venta Books, 1992)
Jocelyn Lukins
Doulton Lambeth Advertising Wares
(Venta Books, 1990)
Jim Murray
The Art of Whisky
(Public Record Office, 1998)
Robert Opie
Remember When
(New Cavendish, 1998)

Victorian Scrapbook
(New Cavendish, 2000)
Mark Reed
Kent Bottles (Sawd Books, 1988)
Willy van Den Bossche
Antique Glass Bottles; Their History and Evolution (1500–1850)
(Antique Collectors Club, 2001)
David Westcott
Advertising Water Jugs (Westcott Publications, 1999)

The following are all pocket-sized Shire Publications:
Bottles & Bottle Collecting 1st ed 1975; 16th print 2000
Clay Tobacco Pipes 1st ed 1979; reprinted 1999
Victorian Chemist & Druggist 1st ed 1981; reprinted 2001

Clubs, shows, & magazines

Regional bottle clubs and annual specialist fairs take place around Britain and in America. Below is a précis of established activities. There may be a modicum of change, so always consult a recent bottle publication featuring definite dates and locations.

UK
The major information source since 1979 has been:
BBR/Collectors' Mart magazine
Elsecar Heritage Centre
Barnsley South Yorkshire
S74 8HJ
tel: 01226 745156

Regional Clubs
A complete list of national clubs with meeting venues, contact names, and addresses is sent out upon joining *BBR/Collectors' Mart* magazine. It covers the following:

Alton, Avon, Berkshire, Brigg and Humberside, Bury, Colchester, Cornwall, Cumbria, Dorset, East Anglia, Exeter, Gloucestershire, Invicta (Kent), Leeds, Northamptonshire, Northern Ireland, Northumberland and Durham, Norwich and District, Oxford, Plymouth, Preston, Reading, Shrewsbury, Somerset and Devon, southwest Wales, South Yorkshire, Surrey, Trent Valley, Warwickshire, West Sussex, Wiltshire, Worcester

BBR magazine also provides a comprehensive listing of related interest clubs and newsletters.

Shows
Throughout the year, a number of established events take place approximately on the same date and month each year:

January: Bletchley; Coddswallop, South Yorkshire
March: Alton, Hants; Spring Extravaganza, Elsecar Heritage Centre, South Yorkshire
April: Aylesbury; Cirencester; Shrewsbury
May: Bridge of Earn, Scotland; Hemel Hempstead; Romsey
June: Bowburn
July: UK SummerNational week-end, South Yorkshire
August: Norwich; Reading
September: Bridge of Earn; Romsey; Tonbridge
October: Autumn Extravaganza, Elsecar Heritage Centre, South Yorkshire; Aylesbury; Leatherhead
November: Alton; Kidlington

BBR magazine features contact names, addresses, times, locations, etc

USA Clubs and shows
Both the following publications provide news and updates on regional bottle club activities across America, and list all the forthcoming coming specialist shows for bottles and related items:

Antique Bottle & Glass Collector
PO Box 180
East Greenville
PA 18041
tel: (+1) 215 679 3068

Bottles & Extras
88 Sweetbriar Branch
Longwood
FL 32750 2783
tel: (+1) 901 372 8428

Websites
www.antiquebottles.com
www.bankscon.freeserve.co.uk
www.fohbc.com (Federation of Historical Bottle Collectors site)
www.fruitjars.com
www.onlinebbr.com

Where to buy & see

The inexperienced collector should start buying from reputable dealers at specialist fairs organized by experienced and established collectors, or regional bottle clubs. Most dealers will readily impart some knowledge and experience about good, and bad, buys. Certainly a visit to any major specialist fair will afford an opportunity to see and meet stallholders and other collectors.

Auction houses may initially sound daunting, but specialists remain the undoubted best source of "fresh to market" material. Here you can generally buy with great confidence, and pay a little more than is comfortable for a dealer to purchase for resale at a profit. Antique shops and fairs, and car boot and garage sales may all be places to pick up an amazing bargain, but you are advised to "learn the ropes" before venturing unwisely down these avenues.

COLLECTORS' CLUBS
See page 60 for an extensive and established platform, and well-priced material.

UK AUCTION HOUSES
BBR Auctions
Elsecar Heritage Centre
Barnsley
South Yorkshire S74 8HJ
tel: 01226 745156
Bonhams (Chelsea)
65–9 Lots Road
London SW10 0RN
tel: 020 7393 3999
Christie's South Kensington
85 Old Brompton Road
London
SW7 3LD
tel: 020 7581 7611
Sotheby's
34–35 New Bond Street
London
W1A 2AA
tel: 020 7293 5000

UK MUSEUMS
Most major and regional museums hold a broad range of bottles, pot lids, and advertising material, though sadly much of it remains in store.

The following display a broad selection of items. Please contact the museums for opening times before travelling.

Coddswallop
Elsecar Heritage Centre
Barnsley
South Yorkshire
S74 8HJ
tel: 01226 745156
Beamish North of England Open Air Museum
Beamish
County Durham DH9 0RG
tel: 0191 3702533

Bass Museum
137 High Street
Burton on Trent
Staffs DE14 1EW
tel: 01283 511000

"How We Lived Then", Museum of Shops and Social History
20 Cornfield Terrace
Eastbourne
East Sussex BN21 4NS
tel: 01323 737143

The Museum of Bath at Work
Camden Works
Julian Road
Bath BA1 2RH
tel: 01225 318348

Castle Museum
York YO1 7ET
tel: 01904 653611

USA AUCTION HOUSES

Glassworks Auctions
PO Box 180
East Greenville
PA 18041
tel: (+1) 215 679 5849

Norman C. Heckler
79 Bradford Corner Road
Woodstock Valley
CT 06282
tel: (+1) 860 928 2271

USA MUSEUMS

National Bottle Museum
76 Milton Avenue
Balston Spa
NY 12020
tel: (+1) 518 885 7589

Index

Page references in *italics* refer to illustrations

advertising items
    breweriana *10*, *11*
    dairy items *14*, *15*
    Doulton *17*, *23*
    ginger beer *22*, *23*
    go-withs *24–5*
    ink bottles *29*
    jugs *54–5*
    leaflets *18*
    mineral waters *36*
Alloa bottles *13*
"Andrew Cameron" cream pot *15*
Ashtead Pottery *55*
"Auld Lang Syne" crock *57*

baby feeders *48*
"E. Bannister" cream pot *15*
"Barnsley Brewery" jug *54*
Barrett & Elers *36*
bathroom collectables *26–7*
Battersea filters *53*
"Bazin's Shaving Cream" lid *43*
bear's grease *42*, *44*
bedwarmers *27*
beer bottles *10*
beer cans *11*
bellarmines *50*
Beswick *17*
"Bewick Brothers" ginger beer *20*
black glass *9*, *12–13*, *58*
"Boots Cold Cream" lid *43*
bottle tops *15*
"Boval" inhaler *49*
"Bovril" *33*
breweriana *10–11*
Brougham, Lord Henry *50*
Buchan Pottery *21*, *32*
"Bungalow Footwarmer" *27*
butter crocks *14*
"Buttercup Cream" pot *14*

"Caley's" matchstriker *11*
care of items *8*, *9*, *25*, *33*
Carltonware *10*, *11*
Carter Ink Co. *29*
case gin bottles *13*

chairs *24*
champagne-shaped bottles *21*, *23*
"The Cheavin Microbe Proof Filter" *52*
"Cheesman's Rat Poison" lid *44*
"Clarke's Miraculous Salve" *38*, *39*
cleaning fluid bottles *16*
codd bottles *7*, *34*, *35*, *36*, *37*, *58*
coffin poison bottles *41*
cold cream *43*
collecting *6–7*, *11*, *29*, *37*, *39*, *58*, *62*
coloured lip bottles *23*, *34*, *35*, *37*
coloured top bottles **23**, *32*
"Comrie & Co." ginger beer *22*
condition *7*, *8*, *12*, *15*, *25*, *38*, *45*, *53*
corn cures *43*
cottage ink bottles *31*
counter trays *49*
cream pots *14*, *15*, *58*
crocks *56–7*

"Daffy's Elixir" *46*
dairy items *14–15*
"Dandy Shandy" showcard *36*
"Dartnel's" ginger beer *22*
Delescot *38*
delft *38*
Dewar's *11*, *54*
"Diabetes Cure" bottle *46*
digging *8–9*, *31*, *39*, *45*
display bottles *10*, *33*
display cabinets *25*
displaying *7*, *25*, *31*, *37*
"The Doctors Stout" ginger beer *21*
"Double Diamond" jug *10*
Doulton *16–17*, *22*, *23*, *53*, *54*, *55*, *56*
"Dr. Nelson" inhalers *49*
"Dr. Rooke's Golden Ointment" *39*
drinks dispensers *17*, *20*
"Dulux" dog *17*
Dunn Bennett factory *55*

"Egyptian Salve" *38*

embossed bottles *13*, *31*, *34*, *37*, *47*
Emmerson man trademark *21*
enamelling *13*
eye baths *48*, *58*

faceted base bottles *37*
fakes see reproductions
"Farrimonds FB" beer can *11*
"Farrars" ink bottles *28*
"Field's Ink & Gum" bottle *31*
fire grenades *18–19*
fish paste pots *42*
"Fisher's Seaweed Extract" bottle *47*
flagons *16*
flasks *50–1*
Fletcher's patent poison bottles *40*
"Forty Second Whisky" crock *56*
Fulham Pottery *22*, *23*

"Gaelic Old Smuggler Whisky" jug *55*
"Galway Bay Whiskey" crock *57*
"Geo. Taylor" mineral water *35*
"George Skey" ginger beer *23*
"Gilbert Rae's Aerated Waters" sign *25*
gin bottles *13*
ginger beer collectables *6*, *9*, *20–3*, *58*
glass ink bottles *30–1*
glossary *59*
go-withs *24–5*
"Goffe & Sons" mineral water *37*
"Golden Eye Ointment" *38*
"Gosnell's Cherry Blossom" toilet powder *45*
"Gosnell's Cherry Tooth Paste" lid *44*
"The Grimwade Pie Funnel" *33*
"Grip Tight" feeder bottles *48*
"Guinness" collectables *11*

hamilton bottles *34*, *35*, *58*
"Handyside's Consumption Cure" bottle *9*
"Hardens Star" grenades *18*, *19*
"Harwood's" ink bottles *29*

"Helsby Creamery" pot 14
hexagonal-shaped bottles 40
"Holloways Ointment" 38
"Horner's" cream pot 14
hot water bottles 27
"HP Sauce" bottle 32
"Hurn's Ginger Beer" bottle 6

"Imperial" grenades 18
"The Improved Pie Funnel" 33
inhalers 49
ink bottles 28–31

"Johnnie Walker" jug 55
"Joseph Gidman" ginger beer 21
jugs 10, 54–5, 58

"Kalamazoo" grenades 19
Keystone Steam Bottling
    Company 37
kitchenalia 32–3

labels 30, 32, 33, 37, 49
lamps 11
Langford, G. F. 41
lavatory disinfectors 26
"Lawrance & Sons" ginger beer
    21
Lee, Carlton H. 40
"Lee's Ointment" 38
Lipscombe & Co. 52
Lloyd George, David 17
"Ludford Ginger" dispenser 20

"Ma & Pa Carter" ink bottles 29
"MacSymons Stores" butter crock
    14
marmalade pots 33
Martin's patent poison bottle 41
matchstrikers 11
Maw & Son 26, 49
"Maw's Lavatory Disinfector" 26
"McNish's Special Whisky" jug 55
"Mew's Beer" can 11
milk bottles 15
mineral water collectables 25,
    34–7
miniatures 16, 22, 46
"Mrs Croft's Ointment" 39
muff warmers 27

Nailsea glass 13
"Nature's Herbal Ointment" 38

novelty items 10, 11, 17, 31

octagonal-shaped bottles 13
ointment pots 38–9
Oldfield pottery 51
onion-shaped bottles 12, 13

"penny pot" ink bottles 28
"Permutit Water Softener" 53
pharmaceutical items 13, 38–41,
    43–9
pictorial items 13, 22, 42, 43,
    44, 45, 51, 57
pie funnels 33
"Player's Navy Mixture" sign 25
poison bottles 40–1
pontil marked glass 34, 36, 46,
    49, 59
"Poor Man's Friend" ointment 38
Portmeirion 27
pot lids 7, 42–5, 58
pottery
    breweriana 10, 11
    dairy items 14
    Doulton 16–17
    ginger beer bottles 21, 22–3
    household items 27, 32, 33
    ink bottles 28–9
    jugs 10, 54–5
    pharmaceutical items 38–9, 43,
        44–5, 48–9
    pot lids 42–5
    water filters 52–3
    whisky crocks 56–7
potties 27
Pratt lids 42, 43
preserve jars 13
"Price's Glycerin" bottle 47

quack cures 46–7

"Radam's Microbe Killer" 47
rat poison 44
"Razorbrite Bath" set 26
"Redruth Brewery Co." ginger
    beer 22
reform flasks 50, 58
"Reliance" bottles 35
reproductions 11, 25, 31, 39,45,
    47, 55, 61
rigaree strips 13
"Rabbie Burns Whisky" crock 57
"Robinson & Co." ginger beer 22

"Rock Blue" bottle 32
Ross & Co. 21

safety 9, 19
saltglaze 22, 23, 27, 28, 51, 58,
    59
samples 16
sauce bottles 32
sealed bottles 12, 13, 59
shaft and globe bottles 12
shaving cream 43
shoe shine boxes 24
shop rounds 49
showcards 11, 36
signs 25, 58
skittle-shaped bottles 20
skull poison bottles 40
slab seals 51
slipware 51
"Spark's Perfect Health" counter
    trays 49
spirit barrels 51
split size bottles 12, 20
stamp dampers 17
"Stiff & Sons" ginger beer 23
"Stohwasser & Winters" bottle 16
stoneware 6, 27, 50–1, 56, 59
stoppers
    chisel head 10
    crown cork 10, 20
    "Crystal" valve 35
    Galtee More patent 21
    wooden plug 36
    see also bottle tops; codd bottles
        "E. B. Storm" ginger beer 23
submarine poison bottles 41
"Sunderland Grant Mackay
    Whisky" crock 56
"Swan Red Ink" bottles 28
"Système Labbe" grenades 19

Tamworth Pottery 23
"Taylors Rolyat Disinfector" 26
"teakettle" ink bottles 31
"Thompson (M. F.)" tooth paste
    lid 45
"Thompson's" ginger beer 20
"Tiger Sauce" bottle 32
tin signs 25
tinglaze 28
tippers for ink bottles 30
toilet powder 45
tooth paste 7, 44, 45

transfers 15, 21, 27, 32, 45, 57
"Trouchet's Corn Cure" lid 43
two-tone items 9, 21, 22,33,58

veterinary flasks 51
"Virago" ink bottles 29
"Votes for Women" ink bottles 29

Wade 55
Waller & Son 38
"Warner's Safe Cure" bottle 46, 58
water filters 52–3
water jugs 54–5
whisky-related items 11, 54–7

Wilson's patent poison bottles 40
wine bottles 12–13, 50
"Woods Areca Nut Toothpaste" lid 7
"Wotherspoon (R.) & Co." pot 33

Acknowledgments

All pictures photographed by Steve Tanner for Octopus Publishing Group Ltd, courtesy of Alan Blakeman/BBR Auctions